Dedicated to my wife Michelle for without her, none of this would be possible. And all our wonderful kids, for without them, life itself would be a very empty place.

Screw It Just Do It

Introduction: Who the hell is Peter Hart? (Page 1)

Chapter 1: Dare To Dream (Page 11)

- Discovering what your goals are
- Finding out why you want to start a business
- Realising you're best at the things you love

Chapter 2: A Rolling Stone (Page 25)

- How to make your business happen
- Getting it going without wasting time
- Taking action and avoiding prevarication

Chapter 3: Stick To What You Know (Page 40)

- Looking in depth at the knowledge you already have
- Identifying the best suppliers and making contact
- Deciding where your customers will come from

Chapter 4: Build Your Foundations (Page 54)

- How to make sure your business is ready to go

- Setting up bank accounts, PayPal, Amazon, eBay accounts – channel unity

- Introduction to business practice basics – accounts, pay etc

Chapter 5: Get online (Page 65)

- How to get your products online and into all the marketplaces quickly and effectively

- Deciding how each product is represented, what to do about imagery and descriptions

- Building your own profile online

Chapter 6: Gain Market Share (Page 82)

- How to get your customers to notice you

- How to get your customers to buy from you

- How to get your competitors' customers to buy from you

Chapter 7: It's Good To Talk (Page 97)

- Keeping customers by regular communication, emails, newsletters, offers, deals

- Maintaining the conversation over time

- Using your existing customer relations to attract new customers

Chapter 8: Get Social (Page 112)

- Building an attractive and effective social media profile

- Discovering what works best on Facebook, Twitter, Instagram, YouTube etc

- Finding out about the unexpected benefits

Chapter 9: Analyse This, Analyse That (Page 125)

- Why Google Analytics might just save your business life

- Measure everything, interpret the results, then take actions to influence those numbers

- Using Google AdWords to boost your business

Chapter 10: The Sun Always Shines On TV (Page 135)

- Me and Duncan Bannatyne – be careful what you wish for

- Staffing your growing business and how to make money through multiple streams of income

- Learn how to recognise the time to sell and making the best exit possible to live your dream

Introduction

Who the hell is Peter Hart?

The chances are you don't know me from Adam. In fact, I'd be a little surprised if you did know me. So why should you pay attention to a single thing I've got to say?

Fair enough, but here's why. These days I have a successful online business selling fancy dress, party gimmicks and magic items. It does all right. Actually, it does more than all right and we turn over millions of pounds a year, more than enough to keep me and my family and plenty to allow us to enjoy some of the things that make life worth living.

But it wasn't always like that. When I left school I didn't have a single qualification to my name and no idea what I was going to do to get by. All I knew was that somehow I had to because nobody else was going to do it for me.

And that is what has driven me all through my life – the need to earn a crust to keep food on the table and a roof over my head. We keep getting told the country is awash with scroungers are cheats, but there are tens of thousands of people just like me out there all working away just to get by. They're good people with lots to offer, the kind of people that get overlooked because they don't cause any trouble.

People keep telling me my story would make a book and here it is. With any luck someone might take something from it – an idea, a thought, a tiny piece of advice – that might open up a different path towards a goal they never knew they had. I don't know if it's a good story, I don't know if I've got any great insight, that's for you the reader to decide, but what I do know is that it's my story and every single word of it is the truth; the whole truth and nothing but the truth.

I was born at midnight on 11 October 1971 to Joyce and George Hart in Hammersmith, London. My dad was a caretaker for the council and my mum had various cleaning jobs in the area. I'm the youngest of six so it was quite a large family compared to the average family these days, but not too uncommon back then.

We lived in a big council house that just about held us all. Even so, sharing rooms and beds was a must, but we didn't mind because that was all we knew. In fact we didn't seem to be in the house very much at all and my main memories as a small child are that I was always out playing in the local streets with the other kids – not like today where we all keep our kids indoors because we're too scared not to.

I've got lots of memories of going on family holidays to Butlins. We would go every year, sometimes twice. A family holiday was something my parents always made sure we had, no matter how tight money was. I really appreciate that now, looking back.

There was always noise though and everything was constantly on the move – someone was rushing in as someone else was dashing out, nothing ever settled for very long. Us kids were always at each other's throats, there were always arguments amongst my older brothers and sisters – we all really gave our mum and dad a hard time and I feel some regret for that now, but maybe it's just the way our family was. Then again, maybe all families are like that.

School, now there's a thing. I didn't suit school very well – or it didn't suit me, I'm still trying to work out which way round it was. My problems at school started when I was about 10 and I started to get picked on, bullied. Things might have been different if it had been nipped in the bud there and then, but it wasn't and because I was going to 'big' school soon, nothing was done about.

The funny thing was, when I first started secondary school, it looked like it had been the right tactic and I got off to a flying start. I was always in the top groups and performed well in tests, with good marks. The teachers were happy, but even then I knew I wasn't. In fact I was downright miserable.

The real issues started when I was about 14. A mate of mine at school, I think his name was Anton, had a job in the butchers in Shepherds Bush and the greengrocers next door said they were looking for someone to help them out. He told me about this and I thought it would give me a way out of all that rubbish at school. So I went along for a chat and got the job, just like that. Bloody brilliant it was.

I can honestly say that decision set me off on a path that I'm still on to this day.

I went to work there in the morning, getting in at about 6am to help open up and trim the veg and set up the displays. Then I had to go off to school and most days I'd be back at the shop straight after school helping them close up and get ready for the next day. I loved it. I felt I was part of something in a way that I never was at school. Inevitably, as the months went on I found I was spending more and more time working at the greengrocers and less time at school.

It wasn't all above board though. The greengrocers didn't mind me being there as I was a good worker and they liked me, but I wasn't exactly completely up front about what I was doing it with my mum and dad. I had to keep my eyes open as mum used to come to the centre to do her shopping so if I was supposed to be at school – and I usually was – I had to be ready to duck behind the counter when she came through!

It's difficult to imagine now, but back in the 80s the school didn't call home or do anything really if you were absent – at least our school didn't – so I managed to get away with it for some time.

But nothing as good as that lasts forever and eventually someone at the school caught on to what I was doing and decided they'd better be seen to be bothered, which is when the letters home started. It wasn't long before mum was being summoned to meetings with teachers and then the local education authority until it finally ended up in court.

I put my poor mum through hell with all the stress of this and now of course I wish I hadn't, but at the time I felt I didn't have a choice except to follow my own course. I wasn't doing anyone any harm, I didn't ask anyone for anything – didn't need to, I had my own money!

I can still hear the magistrate's words. She said that she knew no matter what happened in court there was no way I was going to return to school. Wise lady. I nodded and agreed. Then she said: "Well, by the time this makes its way through the system, you'll be old enough to leave anyway, so we'll leave it at that."

If ever there was a victory for common sense it was then, but I remember being massively surprised at the time.
So that was it, I was out of school and on my own. I can remember a lot of my school friends from back then and thanks to Facebook I'm back in contact with a small number of them. I wonder what they thought when I just disappeared, did they even notice?

It was a huge relief for me of course. And for mum as it turned out. For me it meant that I could go to work every day without having to hide, which was great. I was taking home £100 a week and a big box of fruit and veg on the Saturday after work. I had more money than most my age and was contributing towards the housekeeping at home. Mum knew where I was and, more importantly, knew I was happy. She trusted me to do the right thing and that's something I still have a lot of respect for.

I learned a lot about being in business in that job, but more importantly I picked up a hell of a lot about people while I was there. Mainly I was in the company of adults so I got to see all sorts – from the duckers and divers to the tricksters and skivers. I learned what hard work meant and saw at first hand just how hard you have to work to keep a business on track.

They were important days, some of the best, but I eventually left there in 1989 at the age of 17 to go and work as a bluecoat in Hastings for Haven Holidays. I only worked there for one season before returning to London to live with my parents, but it was a great year and again one that proved to be a very important crossroads in my life.

Back in London though I really started to feel lost. I was lacking direction, drifting, unsure of myself and did not have a clue what I was going to do with my life. I always kept working though, moving from job to job, but never sticking at one thing for very long – I worked in a mechanics, an upholstery unit, loads of different shops, always getting a wage but never really finding my feet. I even had a job making pencils out of twigs!

We've all got skeletons in our closet and I'm no different. There's stuff that happened that doesn't really belong here, it's not the right time and place. Suffice to say I'm no angel and I'm not about to start preaching like one. I'll give anyone a chance, just as people gave me a chance. It's a terrible thing to write someone off and say they'll never amount to anything, so I never have. Perhaps if I get the opportunity to write another book, I'll get those skeletons out for a proper dusting off, but on the whole, I had a great childhood and that's solely down to how hard my mum and dad worked. I have absolutely no doubt of that.

So the 1990s were not an easy time for me, or for many others in fact. There was a recession, people were getting laid off and all the old industries were changing. Suddenly we weren't manufacturing anything in this country, we were a nation of consumers. The dip didn't last long – not like the current one – but it was sharp and made it a tough time to be young.

The thing is I always wanted to have a business, to do something for myself that I could reap the rewards from. I could see other people doing it, but that was the point, it was always something other people did. Back then it wasn't something someone like me did. In those days you were told to get a job and that was that.

It wasn't until I started work at Staples around 2000 that the business world really opened up to me. I got more of a taste of what could be possible and for the first time really started to see how working hard would bring its own rewards. I started out as a general sales associate and within five years had worked my way up to become general manager of the Charlton store in south London.

I met some amazing people there – Dee, Nick, Dave, Woody, Adam and many more, a really great bunch of people, but things were about to change again and I ended up transferring to Poole on the south coast with my wife who was working for Waitrose. By this time we had four kids and not for the first time in my life, money was becoming a real issue. I had to do something, make a move so that I could take care of my family. I couldn't see how to do it without the money coming in from Staples so I had to come up with something I could do in addition to my proper job.

After some searching for ideas, I decided to start a car valeting business. I bought a cheap van and a few bits of equipment, got on a training course for a couple of days and that was it. At last I was in business for myself.

The motivation was most definitely money but on my days off from Staples I was out cleaning cars.

As I got more and more bookings I found I had to work weekends as well as my days off until it reached a point where I had to make the decision I thought had been dreading – do I walk away from a secure monthly wage and a career in retail to take a chance on a business washing cars?

It turned out it was no decision at all and I quit work at Staples the very next day. The decision was easy, very easy.

The fear of not having the safety net of a monthly wage was more than offset by the sense of freedom I had found working for myself. It's very hard to put into words what it feels like to work for yourself. You are, quite literally, your own boss. Nobody's going to tell you to work harder, longer or for less money. You might do all those things, but it will be your decision to do so, nobody else's. All of a sudden when you work for yourself you don't have to explain yourself to anyone. The only targets are those you set yourself, you start and finish work when you like, you can take time off, work extra, start something new, do anything you damned well please.

It is an amazing feeling, the best feeling in the world. And it's something I would recommend everyone should try, at least once.

Of course, all those things are true, you can do whatever you like, but unless you're very fortunate you also have to make a living. All that freedom comes at a price – it's up to you and you alone to earn enough to feed yourself and your family.

So, the car valeting business went well for a couple of years, with lots of regular customers and I was earning quite well, but around this time, my wife and I started trying our luck selling a few bits on eBay. It was approaching Halloween so we bought a box of fancy dress costumes from a wholesaler we found online. The whole lot sold, very fast. We bought a couple more boxes of stock and sold those as well. Then a couple more and a couple more after that and so on until within six months we had a house full of boxes of fancy dress costumes and the car valeting was playing second fiddle to the eBay business.

I quite liked messing around on the computer so I put a little website together to help with the sales and that quickly got up to around £500 a month in sales plus all the eBay sales. It wasn't until we had been doing this for about 18 months that we realised just how big it could be.

And that realisation is really the point of the book.

We've worked incredibly hard to get to where we are today and now we're able to enjoy our life in a way that wasn't possible just a few years ago. It hasn't all been plain sailing, far from it, but we have achieved a hell of a lot and not a day goes by that we aren't grateful for the lives we have.

We're not anything special; we don't have a string of business degrees; nobody told us what to do or gave us any guidance once we were doing it. We've done it all ourselves. And if we can do it, anyone can do it. I really believe this.

Your future is in your hands. If you're unhappy in what you're doing, change it. Don't give up; make that leap. And do it now.

Screw it, just do it!

Chapter 1: Dare To Dream

In this chapter:

- **Discovering what your goals are**

- **Finding out why you want to start a business**

- **Realising you're best at the things you love**

Many people fantasise about running their own business and having the freedom to come and go as they like, taking holidays when they want, buying nice things and having no money worries. The trouble is, a fantasy is all that ever will be. The fact of the matter is you will never work so hard as you will when running your own business. If you're looking for an easy life, being a business owner is not for you, especially in the early stages.

I was just 15 when I decided I'd had enough of school. I'd played truant for the best part of a year in any case so it seemed pretty clear to me that I had better things to do. I'd worked in my local greengrocers in Shepherds Bush before school, during the day on occasion and at weekends. I was paid £100 a week and got to take home a box of free fruit and veg on Saturdays – great pay and pretty good perks for a 15-year-old back in 1987.

I left school early because I thought I didn't need it. I had a job and money in my pocket, the kind of freedom many 15-year-olds could only dream of, so why bother to spend my time at school when I could be earning instead? I didn't see the point of equations, I'd had it up to here with English Literature and what was I learning in History? Absolutely nothing. Honestly, leaving school was a no-brainer at the time, but one I would later come to regret… a little bit at least.

The point is, it pays to think before you act. I swapped my schoolbooks for a weekly wage because I thought I was better off. Maybe I was at the time, but what about further down the line? Every action has a reaction, every cause an effect. Now, I'll never know what might have happened if I'd stayed on at school, knuckled down and got a few qualifications under my belt and to some extent there's not much point losing too much time thinking about it, but at the time I didn't give it a moment's thought. School or a ton a week – what's to think about? Take the money every time.

What I'm trying to say here is that before you rush in and start your own business you need to take a moment to think about the consequences of your actions. And not just in the here and now either, but what will it mean for you in three or four years' time?

I love thinking about a new business, it's an incredibly exciting time and absolutely vital to your future success, but even more important is the time you spend thinking about the most fundamental questions of all. You need to take some time out to be on your own, clear your head and have a good old ponder.

Here are some of the questions you need to have answers for:

Why do you want to start a business?

What is your goal in starting a business?

What are you trying to achieve?

What business do you want to start?

What is the point of your business?

What do you need that business to do for you?

How much time will running your business take?

What are you going to have to give up in order to devote that time to your business?

Can you afford to support yourself and your family if things don't go to plan?

Who is going to make your business happen?

When are you going to start your business?

How is it going to work?

Where will your business be based?

What will be the measure of your success?

OK, so that's just a list of questions, but thinking about them will help you focus on the reality of running your business. You need to not only know what you're doing but why you're doing it. You need to understand your own actions and see where they fit in with your dreams and schemes, your goals. Thinking about these things and knowing the answers to those questions – and many more besides – means you will be working for yourself in every possible sense.

However, not all the answers lie in the answers. I know it sounds confusing, but coming up with decent answers to those questions is just the first step on your way to starting a business, it's not the be all and end all. They're all questions that you should be aware of and have considered answers for, but – and I can't emphasise this enough – *do not let them dictate what you do*.

By acknowledging the above questions and giving serious thought to the answers you will almost certainly recognise a series of potential failure points. These are the things that might go wrong, things that might get in your way, hold you back and even cause you to fail. What you're doing though is creating The Fear. And it's The Fear that can stop you from ever taking the leap into the business world.

In fact, most people will never get past The Fear. They will mistake The Fear for reason and talk themselves out of starting a business. They will use The Fear as an excuse not to attempt new things, or take risks, or push themselves to try harder and work smarter. In short, they will fail to see opportunities for what they are by allowing their lives to be controlled by something that hasn't happened and may never, ever happen. Sounds silly, right? Yes, but we've all done it. That's the power of The Fear.

So, how to avoid The Fear? The only way to conquer The Fear is to confront it, look it in the eye and stare it down. You need to be mentally strong, incredibly determined and absolutely certain of your position. That's why you have to think about those questions and know what the answers are. In that way you will have seen the points of weakness in your plan, you'll know where The Fear comes from and you'll have taken steps to head it off.

Dig down deep and ask yourself why you want your own business.
Is it money? Freedom? Security? Do you need a new challenge? Do you want to help others or to prove something? Maybe you want to save the world? There are more reasons for starting a business than there are fish in the sea, but whatever your reason, make sure it is your reason and nobody else's. You must be brutally honest with yourself, probably more honest than you've ever been and you have to know the reasons behind your answer.

Why do you want your own business?

Get this wrong and your business will fail. The only reason for having your own business is your own reason and yours alone. Trying to live someone else's dream will never work because you simply won't be able to maintain the motivation required for it to be a success. Unless you know what your reason is for having your own business you'll never be able to devote every last drop of time and energy to it because that's what it will need.

Nobody said any of this would be easy. In fact, the absolute opposite is true. Running your own business is hard, hard work. It will nag at your very soul, keep you awake at night and occupy your thoughts from morning to night. But it is also the most rewarding, satisfying and downright fun thing I can think of doing without having to turn the lights off!

Whatever you achieve in other areas of your life nothing feels quite the same as turning a profit from your own hard work. Sweet. And by knowing what your ultimate goal is, you will be able to start up your business in the correct and most efficient way, from the way you structure your business to whom, if anyone, you employ, the jobs they do and how they go about doing them.

OK, let's bring MONEY into play here. While it's true there are millions and millions of different reasons for starting your own business – motivation is a very personal thing – in my experience the most common reason people give for wanting to start a business is MONEY. MONEY, MONEY, MONEY. MONEY. MONEY makes the world go round. MONEY.

To some, it's the evil word that's associated with all the bad things out there such as greed, selfishness, deceit and so on ... MONEY doesn't talk, it shouts.

But MONEY is not a bad word. MONEY can't buy me love, but it can buy me choice. It can buy freedom. With MONEY I have options. I can go left or right, up or down, forward or back, in or out. MONEY means I can help others, be they friends, family members or complete strangers. Being able to do so makes me happy and so it should.

MONEY.

Think a little harder though and for most people, it's not actually about the accumulation or pursuit of MONEY. In and of itself, MONEY doesn't mean anything more these days than a list of numbers on a screen. Even if you have physical MONEY in front of you, what is it but a pile of paper or coins? And what does that really mean? Not much.

But what MONEY can do, now that's something else altogether. That is why I wanted to deal with MONEY at this early stage, to get it out of the way, on the table, up on the wall, wherever you want to put it. People often say MONEY is the reason they want to have their own business, but invariably what they really mean is what they can do with the MONEY they plan on making from their business.

Once you know what your ultimate aim is, why you want your own business, you can start to take the steps that will bring you closer to that goal. Whatever that goal is, be honest about it and keep it at the top of the list. Make sure everything you do brings you a step closer to achieving that goal and if your next action doesn't help you move forward towards that goal in some way, then don't do it. Simple.

That doesn't mean you have to turn into a single-minded monster hell bent on success at any price, but it does mean you have to be tough with yourself and probably more ruthless than you've ever been before. Embrace it, turn it to your advantage and get ready to reap the benefits. Let's be clear though, ruthlessness is not the same as nastiness, it won't make you a fiend it simply means you are able to remain very focused on your agenda.

Being that determined can be a lonely business, but it's your determination to succeed that will make the difference between doing so and not doing so. However, nobody does it alone. Not entirely. You will need the support of those around you – your parents, your other half, your friends, your kids, your business partners. Some people want to go it completely alone, but you will not be able to do this on your own. We're social creatures, we exist as part of a wider society and business is a function of society so that requires other people to be involved in it.

Gather the people you trust the most around you, the ones you feel most comfortable with and the ones you can be sure have your best interests at heart. Discuss everything with them, share your plans and talk about why you are taking whatever action is next. Canvas their opinions and listen to what they say, but do not let their views decide what you do.

The people around you will generally want to protect you and they will raise concerns and identify potential points of failure, but as we discovered earlier *do not let them dictate what you do.*

Your friends, family and close associates are also victims of The Fear. They're frightened of failure – not so much for themselves as for you. They worry about you and they don't want to see you fail so they will be likely to counsel against taking risks. But it's The Fear again, nothing more. So you must be able to bring them into the fold for support and take all the positives from what they have to say, draw strength from their continued backing and use that energy to drive you forward.

Not that you should blindly ignore their opinions, but remember this: unless they are prepared to share in your losses, their motivation for thinking the way they do will be very different to yours. They care about you, they may even be concerned that they'll be the ones that have to pick up the pieces if you fail, but they probably won't understand precisely what is driving your actions.

So far, everything has been quite abstract. You want a business, but what business? You know why you want a business, but what is your business going to be? Once you've decided to go for it, you'll need to decide what you're going to do. Are you going to sell flowers or open a coffee shop? Perhaps you'll start a car cleaning company, or plan weddings, or cut grass... there's an endless amount of things you can start a business doing, so how do you decide what to do?

The best advice is to start with what you know. Look at what you are currently doing and think about the job you have mostly done over the years. What hobbies do you have? What resources are available to you? What would you need to get going? How long could it last? What do you need to do first?

Looking inwards at what you already know always means there is less to learn so you should be able to grow much faster than having to learn something from scratch, but ultimately your business should be something you love doing. You are going to be spending a ridiculous amount of time doing this thing so you will need a relentless drive and absolute passion for it. Without this emotional attachment, it will quickly become just another job to you and not the dream that set you on this journey.

We all know what it's like to encounter poor service from someone who clearly doesn't care about the job. If you're anything like me, you'll go somewhere else next time, somewhere that does care about you. Bad attitudes usually come from the top down. If you are going to have your own business, your enthusiasm for it will rub off on your team and that in turn will translate to your customers. If your customers like what they see, get what they want from your goods and services and feel valued by your business, not only will they keep coming back but they will be much more likely to tell others about your business as well.

All of which means your business is greatly increasing its chances of success.

It's probably a good time to point out that unless you're very lucky, your business may not make any money in the first and maybe even the second year of trading. It's a harsh reality, but a reality nonetheless. Making a new business pay from a standing start is almost impossible and even less likely if you actually price up your own time that you spend on getting it off the ground. If this happens to you, stay focused and try not to worry about it, you will still be able to enjoy some of the benefits of running your own business – the freedom, the sense of purpose, the sheer joy of being your own boss and doing something you love – but don't expect to be able to draw a decent wage until the third or fourth year of being in business.

So long as you work smart and keep going through all the challenges, you'll make it.

Having left school and gone to work at the greengrocers I spent a lot of my younger years drifting from job to job. I worked in a garage, as an upholsterer, in a sweet shop, I was at a company that made pencils from twigs, I worked in a take-away, I was even a holiday park entertainer down in Hastings for a few months in 1989. The fact is, I had no idea what I was doing or where I was going, I just felt that as long as I was working everything would be fine.

It's not a bad approach to life – far better than sitting on your arse playing video games and waiting for the world to drop a living in your lap – and I had a great laugh, but it does lack a certain focus. And if there's one thing you need when you have your own business, it's focus. You need to pay attention to every last little detail of your business, from the overall plan and business strategy, right down to your listing in business directories and the typeface on your business card.

If you can demonstrate to your customers and members of your team that you're prepared to sweat the small stuff they'll have far greater faith in your ability to deliver a great service and lead the business in the right direction.

That way of thinking didn't really hit me until I found myself working for Staples, the office supplies superstore chain. That was where my passion for business was ignited. Suddenly, lots of things started to make sense, all these thoughts started to crystalise and pretty quickly I realised that the reason I had struggled so much over the years working for other people was because my talents lay elsewhere.

I lasted around five years with Staples, progressing from a humble store associate to general manager of the Charlton branch. All the time I was learning more and more about the actual business of business, about how things worked, about the law, about managing people, about customers and fellow members of staff. I knew things would have to change but I never really had a plan until one day, out of the blue, I quit ... just like that. That day it hit me, I had to get out and get out now.

Funnily enough, that was also the moment that I realised I had a plan I knew what I was going to do.

I'd picked up an old van a few months earlier and had been doing some car valeting on my days off and at weekends just for a bit of extra cash. I enjoyed the work, meeting lots of different people and being able to do a great job for them. Before too long I was actually turning car valeting jobs down because I didn't have the time as I was still employed by Staples – my career job was getting the way of my career, if you see what I mean.

It was obvious what had to happen next – I had to go full-time I'd be a self-employed car valet. More than that, I'd be the best self-employed car valet. So I left, I took the plunge and walked away from a job with prospects that was paying me a very good wage. I remember saying one day to my wife, 'That's it, screw it, let's just do it.' And we did. But from the very first day I absolutely loved running my own business, I was hooked on working for myself. My journey had begun.

Looking back I wouldn't change a thing about what I did and the way I went into business for myself, but that's just me. It worked. I was lucky. However, I would always advise anyone who is thinking seriously about starting their own business to take a moment to think about it properly and make a plan. Whatever your goal is – in life, in love, in business – write it down, type it, print it off and stick it up on your wall. Look at it every day and don't let anyone or anything distract you from it. Never lose sight of your goal.

There will be many people who, for whatever reason will try to hold you back. Some will be out to burst your bubble because it exposes their own shortcomings, others will think they are trying to protect you from failure, but there's no such thing as we'll see later on. However they dress it up, they're still trying to take your goal away from you. Don't let them do it. Stay focused on what you know is the right path for you. You may well encounter setbacks along the way, but each one brings you another step closer to your goal. You will only fail if you quit.

THREE TOP TIPS

DO
Define clear goals, get them down on paper and look at them every single day. Make sure you fully understand *your* reasons for starting a business.

A PITFALL
It's very easy to start fighting fires in the early days, stay true to your goals at all costs. The people around you may try to hold you back, stay focused.

DON'T
Quit. Never, ever, ever, ever give up. It's an obvious one, but most people quit before they've even really started. It's going to be hard in the early days, but just keep on pushing and fighting for what you want and you'll get there in the end.

Chapter 2: A Rolling Stone

In this chapter:

- **How to make your business happen**

- **Getting it going without wasting time**

- **Taking action and dealing with problems**

So you've worked out what your goals are and what your business is going to be, now it's time to make your business happen, to get you off the starting line and out into the big wide world. There's excitement at every step of this process – I told you it would be fun – but also danger. This is the single most important time for any business and the most common time that new businesses fail.

Remember what I said about The Fear? Well, by this time The Fear will be gnawing away at you, eating up your energy and your confidence. The Fear will plant a myriad of worries in your head and you'll do the rest. What if you fail? What if your idea is rubbish? Who's going to want to buy from you? How will anyone know about you? What if the moon is made of cheese and the sky is about to fall in? Don't worry, you'll be giving yourself all kinds of reasons to not take that all-important first step and actually go into business on your own. You must silence that nagging voice in your head, remember you are doing this for a reason and stay focused. This is when you have to be strong, stronger than you've ever been. Before I finally quit my job, turning my back on the security of a wage each month and started to run my first business valeting cars I was very scared. Petrified.

Absolutely terrified. Every negative scenario was going through my head and with four young kids at the time I kept asking myself if I was about to make the biggest mistake of my life. I was lying awake at night going over all kinds of possible failures if I got to sleep I'd wake up afraid it was all going to go horribly wrong, but I knew I had to hang on to my dream.

I knew we could get by on my monthly wage from Staples, but I also knew that it wasn't enough to give my family the kind of opportunities that I didn't have as a kid growing up. Getting started in business at all was only down to the fact that I had an overwhelming hunger for a better life for my family. Without that I may not have made the leap, that vision was what gave the strength to silence the doubting thoughts I kept having. I knew if I held my nerve I could pull it off, on one level I had such confidence, but equally I kept coming up with new ways to make me doubt myself almost as if I was subconsciously trying to give myself a way out of it.

The funny thing is, the day after I quit, the relief was amazing. Exhilarating. I was high as a kite! I'd decided the day I was going quit, tomorrow!. I knew I had the right reasons for doing it, I felt a sixth sense that everything was going to work out, but it still took all my mental strength to push me over the line. And then I did it, I handed in my notice and I was out. Free.

All of a sudden it felt as though I was in a very different world. Nothing was the same any more everything seemed brighter, clearer, sharper than before. I'm not a spiritual person by any means, but I knew that things were going to be changing for the better very soon.

At last I was my own boss, setting my own agenda, doing things my way. By not being an employee anymore, I felt much more in control. I was very aware of the hard work that was in front of me, not to mention no more paid holidays or sick pay, if I didn't work, I didn't earn, but I loved the freedom and power that gave me. I was now driving my own life and nobody was going to change that.

It's difficult to explain to somebody who has never done it, but stepping away from a job or a career in which you have decent pay, security and prospects – all the conventional things that employment advisors tell you are essential to a happy life – and leaping into a world in which you have none of those things is a real buzz. Of course there's an element of danger, but that only adds to the excitement. I got so much energy from making that decision and then acting on it that I hit the ground running when I came to start working for myself full-time. I knew what I had to do, could hardly wait to get started and went at it like a mad thing.

All of which worked out fine… for me. A few years down the line, with a more experienced head on my shoulders, whenever I'm asked for advice about getting started in business I still urge people to take time to plan, think about it and find out as much as you can about running your own business from the people that really know – the people than run their own businesses.

But all the planning in the world is a complete and utter waste of time unless you actually get out there and get started. You can have the best plan in the world, but until you act on it, what does it mean? A plan only ever pays off if you're brave enough to take action. Once you do put that plan into action you'll very quickly learn another big truth about running your own business – the plan won't actually work!

That's right, all that planning you did, you may as well bin it, because the real business world is nothing like people make it out to be in college courses, advice centres, distance learning packages or reality TV shows. Things happen in the real world that nobody could have seen coming. Every single day you'll get thrown a curve ball that you couldn't possibly have worked out a plan for and even if you did have a plan for how to deal with it, when push comes to shove, the plan would be wrong. The real world works a lot faster than you think, it's totally unpredictable and sometimes it's downright weird. But, if you bother to make plans, think about your business and work things out in advance you will be used to thinking in a certain way. You'll have created the mental pathways for your thinking to follow that are essential if you are to work towards your ultimate goals. If you're used to thinking in those terms you'll be well prepared to deal with problems and unforeseen circumstances that the real world will chuck at you when you're least expecting it.

What's more, it may not sound like it, but it's great fun! No two days are ever the same, there's a constant thrill in everything you do and when you've worked hard you reap the rewards. Eventually.

One thing I did learn very early on though – and it's well worth passing on here – is never take advice on your business from anyone who's business is to offer advice. You'll be surprised how many people are out there, especially with the explosion of Twitter and Facebook, just waiting to take advantage of you and charge you a fortune for the privilege of listening to their half-baked business theories. They'll tell you what you should be doing, they'll tell you how you should be doing it, they'll tell you where you should be doing it and for whom, but when you look into how they gained this incredible business insight, you'll find their credentials are sorely lacking. They may have some qualifications, but they've invariably had next to no experience of running a business in the real world.

Only listen to people that have done what you're trying to do and you won't go far wrong. We are the ones who know how it feels to run a business because that's what we've done with our lives. When business people sit down and write books like this it is because they've reached a point in their lives where they've achieved some understanding of their success and now it's time to share some of that success with people that are only beginning their story. We've all had some help along the way and if there's a chance to help others in some way it's only right that we should.

Before your business goes live on the first day there are some practical tasks that you'll have to get done first.

You need to formally set up your business and decide on a business structure that will decide what you are required to do by law, such as the taxes you'll have to pay, what paperwork you need to get started and your responsibilities if you make a loss.

The main types of business are:

Limited company

A limited company is a self-contained business run by its directors and is responsible as a company for everything it does. Its finances are separate to your own personal finances. Any profit it makes is owned by the company, which can then share its profit with its shareholders. If you pay yourself a salary as a director of your limited company you must pay tax and National Insurance and fill in Self Assessment tax return every year.

Partnership
You share personal responsibility for your business with your business partner or partners. You also share all the business profits with your partner(s). That means you are responsible for any losses your business makes and for anything it buys. You must nominate a partner to keep business records and manage tax returns. They must register with HMRC and submit an annual partnership Self Assessment tax return. You must pay tax and National Insurance and fill in Self Assessment tax return every year.

Sole trader
If you're running your business as an individual you keep all profits after tax, but are personally responsible for any losses or purchases. You also have to keep all business records and register with HMRC as a sole trader. You must pay tax and National Insurance and fill in an annual Self Assessment tax return.

All business expecting to take more than £81,000 a year must register for VAT with HMRC and submit a quarterly VAT Return and payment. Registering also allows you to claim back VAT on certain items bought and charge VAT to your clients.

Before your business starts trading you'll also need to open a bank account and find an accountant. You might look at setting up a merchant account with your bank and you'll certainly need to open a PayPal account and set up eBay and Amazon accounts if you're planning on trading online.

This is what I mean about planning. You'll have to think about whether or not you'll need an office or warehouse, or some other kind of storage facility. Do you need a vehicle? What about machinery and tools? Are you going to work from home or share a space with someone else?

The Data Protection Act 1998 requires every business and organisation that processes and stores personal information to register with the Information Commissioner's Office (ICO) for data protection. That means if you keep information about clients you may need to register with the ICO to comply with the law and protect your business and their personal details.

These are just some of the tasks that have to be done to enable you to trade. Some of them you are legally obliged to do and we'll look in detail at those later on, others are things you need to be aware of and think of doing if not now then possibly in the future.

There are some contacts that you'll need to get things off the ground and set up so that you're ready to start trading, in the back of this book.

The key point about all of this is to just get started. Get doing stuff. It really is as simple as that. You've got something to sell, name your price, sell it and record your first sale. Easy. Trading is no different to all the other stuff, the admin, now that you're working for yourself, if you don't do it, it don't get done. So knuckle down and crack on.

More questions…

Is there a right or a wrong way to start a business? What is the very first thing you should do? Well, without knowing it, you've probably already done it. In reality most businesses don't have a grand opening, a Year Zero, first day moment, they tend to evolve into being over a period of time. A bit like my car valeting business, it was just the odd weekend job at first, but that became every other weekend, then every weekend, then a few weekday evenings as well, then my day job started to get in the way of my part-time job and something had to give. All of a sudden you'll find yourself working full-time for yourself without ever having made a conscious decision to start a business.

This is great don't fight it. There's no need. It all works out in the end.

However, there are times when a little forethought and prior knowledge would have gone a long way. That's the reason for writing this book really. How you start your business is entirely up to you, but there are a few things I wish had been said to me when I was starting out that I thought I'd put out there to say to others so they can avoid some of the pitfalls and setbacks I experienced along the way and improve their chances of success.

Fun Fancy Dress, my fancy dress business, has been going for more than seven years now and it's going very well indeed thank you. But when I look back over all the choices and decisions we made, all the mistakes and wasted money, if I knew then what I know now I'm certain that we could knock five years off that development time.

Here are some basic points:

- Cash is king. Don't spend a single penny unless it is going to increase your revenue.

- Know your suppliers. Never buy anything from companies that cold call you within the first couple of years, they will take advantage of your naivety and you'll never get a good deal.

- There are 24 hours in every day. Get six hours sleep and work for the remaining 18. This is a must for the first year.

- Be yourself. Never copy what other people are doing. A business may look like a great success, but you have no idea if they're actually failing. It's a grim fact, but most businesses do fail.

- Customer service should be your main focus. Happy customers are your biggest source of sales, your most effective advert and your best marketing tool. Do whatever is necessary to keep your customers happy.

- Don't hide. Collaborate with other similar companies, get yourself known in your industry sector, get out there and be seen about.

Each of those points is probably worth a chapter in itself, but if you think about it they're all pretty obvious. The thing about running a business, even with everything in your own control, ultimately you are at the mercy of the public. If you are going to succeed you are going to have to convince the people out there to spend their hard earned money with you. And if they're spending their money with you, they have every right to expect you to be thankful. The customer may not always be right, but even if they're not always right, they should always win.

If you win a dispute with a customer, you lose a customer.

As an employee, even a senior employee, there is always someone in a more senior position you can go to for a decision. If you can't make up your mind it's OK because you can just kick the problem along the line and get someone who earns more money than you work it out. But running your own business means the buck stops with you, there's nobody to go to for a decision.

You have to make sure you keep the ball rolling, keep all the plates spinning. There are no half days or long weekends away, no crafty afternoons, no flexi-time, no late starts and no early finishes. Your whole being, everything that you are must be 100% focused on achieving your goal, from the minute you wake up to the minute you go to sleep. It's a tall order and there's no point in pretending otherwise, but staying that motivated is not easy, it's probably the hardest work of all the hard work you put in. The way to deal with it is to build little rewards into your goal planning routine, little targets that trigger a special treat when you hit them – a night out when you make a certain number of sales for example. It doesn't have to be anything big, but just doing something purely for your own enjoyment from time to time re-energises you and can make all the difference the next time the going gets tough.

When I get to my office now, the first thing I do is download all my emails, somewhere in the region of 150 or so each morning and then maybe another 70-80 throughout the day. This usually generates a lengthy list of tasks which I allocate to members of the team where required and then grab a quick update from the warehouse about the previous day's performance and any issues. I'll then most likely go and sweep the warehouse or get the vacuum out. Just because it's your business, it doesn't mean you're too good to do any job that needs doing. You're no Lord Sugar (yet) so in the immortal words of Ali G, keep it real!

In fact, sweeping the floor is great way of calming my head down so I can hear myself think. It's not a job that requires a lot of concentration so it's a good place to order my thoughts and recognise a few ideas – I've had some of my best and most successful ideas when I've been sweeping the floor.

Working for yourself and running your own business it is vital that you keep innovating, keep coming up with new ways of doing things, new lines, new systems, new ideas – your head needs to be an ideas factory working at full capacity. The saying that a rolling stone gathers no moss is very true in the world of business. Don't wait for problems to arise that need solving, go and look for them. Believe me, you'll find plenty of them and then you can fix them before they become serious difficulties that knock your business off track.

Once you're up and running it's very easy to fall into the trap of sitting back and basically letting the business run itself. I can understand why people do it because I've felt like doing it myself. You've been working 18 hours a day seven days a week for months on end and, not to put too fine a point on it, you think you've earned a rest. It's true, you have, you've been working like crazy just to get your business off the ground and now you could do with a breather. Huge mistake, you'll get up one day and BANG!, your bank account is closed, or PayPal has limited your account, or eBay has suspended you.

That could spell disaster for a lot of businesses, but things like that can and do happen to most of us at some point and the business owner who's taken their eye off the ball will suddenly find their business has ground to a halt. You have to be ready for anything at any time, that way you can make sure your business is ready to recover when the unthinkable does happen and, even more importantly, minimise the risk of it closing you down.

It's not my job to put anyone off starting their own business, but we all need to be aware of the stuff that's not on the government websites or in the leaflets you can pick up at the bank or the Job Centre and in the early months of running your business, you'll come across so many problems to the point when you begin to wonder if it's all worth it. At that point, slap yourself hard, look at that goal stuck up on your wall and get back to work. Of course it's worth it!

I remember one particularly grisly horror story not long after I started Fun Fancy Dress. It was a very busy Halloween, we had hundreds of orders coming in every day through Amazon. Ordinarily that would be great news – plenty of orders, plenty of business, plenty of revenue and so on. The trouble was the orders built up so quickly we didn't have the resources in place to ship that many orders each day. We kept going, working all the hours available round the clock packing parcels, shipping parcels, packing more parcels, but we just couldn't keep up. We were selling too much!

This is potentially a bigger issue than not selling enough. As you'd expect Amazon is very protective of its brand – rightly so – and it wasn't long before it stepped in and suspended our account, froze our funds from the sales and denied access to those funds for 90 days. That was that, overnight the business was on the verge of falling apart. Our cash flow was a mess due to the frozen money so we had problems paying our main supplier and we had had no choice but to let quite a few customers down. That of course meant they would almost certainly never use us again. It was a mess, a Halloween from hell, and all brought about through a lack of proper planning on our part.

We were nearly ruined by selling too much. It took nearly a year, but after many talks with Amazon, showing them our new inventory systems and improved postage and warehouse systems we were eventually allowed back. What a relief. We learned a lot during that year and thankfully nothing like that has ever happened again with Amazon. (There are loads of other horror stories, of course, but we'll come to those a bit later!)

There are problems of all shapes and size out there just waiting to bite you on the arse one day. You can anticipate some problems, in which case, make sure you have solutions ready, but most of the problems you'll encounter you won't even have thought possible. I certainly didn't know it was possible to ruin a business by selling too much – until it very nearly happened to me. But unless you realise that things like this can happen, then you don't know to prepare your business for the worse.

It would make me very happy if anyone about to start their own business is able to learn from my mistakes. Hopefully you'll see why it's worth knowing what capacity you have to deal with emails, phone calls, processing orders and shipping items.
Whatever tasks you have to do to make your business work must be stress tested to the point of failure. Then, when your business does take off, you'll know exactly what you're capable of and where to direct any extra effort and resources.

THREE TOP TIPS

DO
Get on with it. Just do it. The perfect time is always right now. The more you plan and talk about doing it, the less likely you are to actually get on and do it.

A PITFALL
You cannot and should not try to plan for every scenario. If your business is selling, then get selling. It won't be perfect right away, so stop trying to make it perfect.

DON'T
Never stop changing. If you find the going easy, you're probably going downhill. Don't ease up – change, challenge, refine, improve.

Chapter 3: Stick To What You Know

In this chapter:

- **Looking in depth at the knowledge you already have**

- **Identifying the best suppliers and making contact**

- **Deciding where your customers will come from**

I left school when I was 15, without a single qualification to my name. Not that I didn't learn anything while I was there, I learned lots of things it's just that I haven't got a piece of paper that shows my knowledge was tested at the time. Regurgitating knowledge is one thing, but there's a world of education that lies beyond text books and that kind of education doesn't finish when you leave school or college, it's lifelong learning – much of it by trial and error.

Nearly every decision I make today is based upon mistakes I've made, not from knowledge I've only gained by doing a course or taking an exam. They say we only really learn from our mistakes and it's very true. Every lesson has a price, some of them higher than others, but if you're willing to pay the price then you can learn a lot of lessons.

No matter how old or young you may be, you will have learned so many things in the course of your lifetime many of which you may not even be aware of. It's all knowledge, the stuff we know. That's how we get through each and every day. We recognise certain situations and circumstances because we've already dealt with them. We know how some things work because we've encountered them before. It's knowledge and knowledge as they say, is power.

Let's find out what you know. If you're reading this there's a fair chance you'll be interested in starting your own business, probably in e-commerce, and you may well want to do that because you've already worked for someone else.

So let's say you've had a few jobs in the past. Get a piece of paper and write them all down, starting with the first one. Then under each job, write what your job actually involved doing. Do this for all the jobs you've had. Now look for common themes, perhaps sales play a big part in all your jobs, maybe it was customer service, maybe it was cleaning. It doesn't matter what but you will see a common theme running through them.

This is where you should focus your efforts when deciding what business you are going to start. Whatever you find is your area should be what you place at the core of what you plan to do.

For me it was sales. Every job I had basically came down to selling products and services. In fact there aren't many jobs or businesses that don't boil down to sales at some point. It's a simple enough equation – if you make something, you need to sell it to make money to make a living. And if you need to sell it there is always an element of having to 'make' sales in order to sell more, or to make sure people buy from you and not your competitors.

Not everyone is able to make things, but we can make a living by buying things at one price and selling at a higher price. We provide a service in that makers know they can bring their goods to us and we'll sell what they've made to our customers. Sellers provide a hugely important service to makers as well as buyers and where does most selling take place these days? Online, of course. There are millions and millions of sales outlets on the internet and while there is no escaping that a website is ultimately where you want your sales to come from, you'll also need to get on to the big platforms such as eBay and Amazon. That's where you will find your buyers.

But for them to have anything to buy, first you've got to find someone to supply it.

You're going to need suppliers.

This will present you with some problems. If you've ever dealt with distributors or wholesalers before, you'll know the restrictions or terms they trade under can have a huge impact on how effectively you'll be able to get your business growing fast, if at all. So when it comes to selecting suppliers, you should ask some key questions:

1. What is the Minimum Order Quantity (MOQ)?

The MOQ is the smallest number of a single product or group of products you can order from a supplier. For example, let's say you intend to sell hats. The supplier may say that you have to buy their hats in quantities of three or more, or maybe they have to be purchased in 12s. This will have a huge impact on cash flow and your ability to store the product, especially for a new business. At this stage you don't know if you're going to sell 12 hats a month or one every three months, so how do you know what to order?

There's no easy answer, but remember what I said about every job or business will eventually come down to sales. Suppliers also need to make sales to survive. They need to make sales to you. You are their customer. Talk to them, tell them your situation, explain what you'd like them to do for you and let them see if they can accommodate your request.

Ideally, as a new business you want to be dealing with the suppliers that will process single item orders, or those that will allow you to return unsold items within a certain timescale, known as Sale or Return. There are lots of suppliers out there, all charging different prices on different terms for the same goods. It can be bewildering, but keep talking, build relationships and see what deals you can make. Sales are vital to all businesses, but so is cash flow and you don't want to tie up a lot of cash in stock at such an early stage of the business. Believe it or not suppliers will understand the situation you're in as it's not so very different to their own. Give them a chance to impress you'll be surprised at what deals you can get just by asking.

2. Will they give you a credit account?

It's very common for suppliers to sell you their products, but not ask for payment until a certain number of days later, usually 30 days. There are no hard and fast rules about this, but you might need to pay upfront for the first couple of orders to build that trust. Like so many things in business, such arrangements are built on relationships. If your supplier sends you the right goods on time and at the right price, you know you can rely on them to do so. Equally, if you pay your bills promptly and make regular orders your supplier will come to view you as a valued and trusted client.

Credit accounts are a vital service for new businesses and suppliers know it. Having a line of credit can be great for growing your business because it gives you the time from receiving the products to selling them before you have to pay. Suppliers will want to minimise their risk in offering credit to a new and untried business so don't be surprised if they limit the credit available to you and make sure you are aware of and fully understand any charges your supplier might make (ideally there won't be any) or having a credit account. Also, be clear about what happens if you don't pay on time.

New businesses have to be careful with credit and there are some pitfalls to watch out for. Most importantly, and every bit as obvious as it sounds, you have to pay. There is always a reckoning and you have to settle your bills with suppliers the same as your customers have to settle theirs with you. Getting cash flow wrong at any stage of your business is the quickest way to fail so remember that if you've got a 30 day account, over those 30 days you'll need to keep some cash aside ready to pay that invoice when it arrives. Your supplier will soon cut you off if you keep paying invoices late.

As useful as credit is my advice is always the same – if you don't need the credit, don't take it. Pay cash for your stock whenever you can. It keeps things simple and means there's no shock when that forgotten invoice turns up in your inbox. Getting into debt is something you should always try to avoid, although once your business gets to a certain size, you'll find it harder and harder not to use credit but by then you should be in a better position to manage it.

3. Do they charge to deliver to you and how long does delivery take?

Buying something is all very well, but what if the goods have to come from some distance away? What if you want more than you could reasonably carry on your own? You are going to need a delivery service and, depending on what it is you are buying, you may need a specialist. All costs that you are going to have to build in to the price you sell at to your customers.

But something as simple as a small delivery charge can soon add up to many hundreds of pounds if not more and can be avoided if you choose your suppliers carefully.

The first rule of thumb here is that you shouldn't be paying your suppliers anything for delivery if you can avoid it. This is generally fine if the suppliers are based in the same country as you, in fact they'll probably make a selling point out of free delivery, but it becomes considerably more difficult when importing goods from overseas. Make sure you get a clear breakdown of delivery charges before you place your order. Find out how much it costs and how well protected the delivery is.

Another very important factor is how long the stock takes to get from your supplier to your business. You should aim to only use suppliers that can offer you a next day delivery as this will enable you to provide a much faster fulfillment rate without having to hold the stock yourself – a huge benefit to your business.

4. Can you return faulty products to your supplier?

There's nothing worse than buying something, taking it home ready to use it and then finding out it's faulty and won't work properly. It's frustrating, irritating and massively inconvenient. Of course an understating retailer who will replace it without a quibble can offset some of the negativity in a display of quality customer service, the kind that you should be aspiring to extend to your customers.

And the kind of customer service your supplier should apply to you. It's pretty much guaranteed that at some point you will receive faulty products back from your customers. It's not a pleasant fact, but it is a fact of life I'm afraid. Being able to return these faulty goods to your supplier means you won't need to take the hit on the price of the item.

However, some suppliers have different ways of handling returns. Some offer credit notes on future orders and some will offer discounts on the original purchase so long as you never return anything to them and deal with the faulty items yourself. Find out how your suppliers prefer to deal with this situation and factor it into your decision making when selecting your suppliers.

5. What are your supplier's best prices and how can you get them?

Everyone wants the best deal, but what is the best deal? Price is always a factor, but it's not the only consideration and you will also need to think about terms, delivery timescales and returns policies as well.

That said, suppliers will often have price breaks or different price levels that are dependent on how much stock you buy, how often and how much you spend over the year. It's not always possible (and rarely easy) to compare like with like, but shop around and you'll soon discover there are many different ways of pricing goods. Ultimately though you want to know what a supplier's very best prices are and what you have to do to get them. Stick to your guns and pin them down on this point because it will have the biggest impact on any profit you're going to make.

Saving just one per cent of cost can increase your profit by as much as a ten per cent rise in sales, but if you're not your supplier's biggest customer negotiating a discount can be tricky. As ever, don't adopt a confrontational stance, talk to the supplier and explain your position to them. Give them some different options such as suggesting increased volumes for the existing price rather than a straight discount, you'll be encouraged to find there's almost always a reasonable solution to be arrived at.

And if you don't get your way, keep your cool, don't take it personally and shop around to see what their competitors will do for you. Your suppliers are in a similar position to your own – they need customers just like you do.

No business can succeed without customers and understanding exactly who your customers are, where they come from, what they need and how they use your goods is key to being successful. If there's one thing you can be sure of it's that your future customers are currently buying from someone else, so your first task is to give them a reason to buy from you instead.

Every business is about pleasing customers, meeting their needs and desires at prices they can afford. Only then will they develop into loyal, life-long customers and, in the final analysis, yield a healthy return on the investment made in them and in the products they need. You might think the best way to get new customers and keep them is to be the cheapest. In actual fact, the biggest mistake you can make here is to think that by being the cheapest, you will sell the most. You might sell the most for a short period of time, but those customers that shop on price alone are a fickle lot and they'll soon be chasing the cheapest price to someone else's door. And even if it were true that being cheapest is the way to go, selling the most is not necessarily the best thing for your business. Lower selling prices inevitably generate smaller margins so you need to sell far more just to stand still in business terms. It's important to remember that your new business has limited resources and capabilities so you don't want to be swamped with orders and not have enough time, money or stock to process them. You have to focus on getting the foundations right first.

When starting out selling online, platforms such as eBay and Amazon can play a vital role in generating sales. Not only are they tried and trusted brands in their own right, but they have a ready-made pool of willing customers eager to spend their money and used to doing so on that platform. People feel comfortable about shopping on platforms such as eBay and Amazon, so products that are featured there assume a level of kudos they might not otherwise have. This is not to be under-estimated and by offering a good product at a fair price, you can get your business off to a great start.

However, these sales platforms have many strict rules that you must follow. We'll come to those a bit later, but they are part of the reason why your ultimate goal is to get people buying from your own website. The likes of eBay and Amazon charge a fee per sale that is generally in the region of 20%. They can also insist on huge discounts if they are to stock your products so you can see the advantages of getting the customers purchasing direct from you.

Nobody in business doubts the importance of having a credible online presence, but it doesn't stop there. It's not enough simply to have a website, it's about how easy your web platform is to find on the worldwide web. By the end of 2014 experts are predicting there will be one billion active websites on the web – that's an incredible number. It is reckoned that about two billion people use the internet so that's one website for every two users. Phenomenal.

Google accounts for just under 90% of UK search engine visits and more than a third of all visits to websites are generated through organic searches on platforms like Google, Bing and Yahoo. More than three-quarters of web users never go past the first page of search results.

Now we all know statistics can be used to prove almost anything you like, but even so it's hard to dispute the importance of getting your website to feature prominently on Google. And because it's important it can also be incredibly difficult to achieve and there is a whole area of expertise that's dedicated to Search Engine Optimisation purely and simply to boost Google rankings.

We'll take a closer look at digital marketing in all its forms later on, but for now here's a few key tips to getting your site noticed by Google:

- Make sure you have an active Facebook page and use your Twitter account regularly. Google loves social media and will notice you using it. This in turn will help your ranking.

- Keep content on all platforms fresh, useful and up to date. Make sure you're the first to post about new products in your sector.

- Google will detect the most unsophisticated attempts to inflate your visibility. Do not post links to your website on every forum you can find, this will not help and may even result in you being kicked off Google ranking altogether, which would be disastrous.

- Be a human! Obvious enough I suppose, but you'd be surprised. When you post information on your website, use normal everyday language, the kind of thing you'd say to your friends and family. Despite what some may say, it is not a good idea to try to pack content full of keywords in an effort to trick Google.

- It's impossible to under-estimate the importance of Google, but there are other search engines such as Bing, Yahoo and many others. In fact, for the last few months Google's market share of UK search engine visits has actually been *falling* while Bing has been on the up.

Knowing where your customers come from, where they go and what they do enables you to target them and talk to them. You're nothing without them so keep in touch with your customers by sending them an email – once a month is fine – updating your Facebook page, tweeting regularly, posting new photos on Instagram, whatever it takes really to make you and your business part of their daily lives.

This isn't something you should be thinking about doing because it sounds like a good idea, this is something you *must* be doing. At the end of the day if you don't do it, your competitors definitely will. You need to be in and amongst their lives so your business shows up when they check Facebook activity, your tweets have something fun, interesting and useful to say – maybe you use Twitter to distribute special one day only offers, or you have a seasonal promotion on Facebook, or a special email discount.

Customers are normal people just like you and me, so you need to stay connected to your customers in the same way you stay connected to your friends and family. And just like your friends and family you are aiming to build a community with them, give them a reason to like you and your company and they'll come to you rather than your competitors.

It's often the simple things that can make the biggest impact, like always responding to posts. So many businesses companies miss this, but it's the attention to detail that willing customers always notice. They want to buy from companies that have their fingers on the pulse and that means social media. You need to be all over your Facebook, Twitter, Instagram and LinkedIn accounts with special competitions, free advice, product news, funny stuff that happens at work, the kind of things that people want in their digital lives.

Not only will all this activity bring you to the attention of new customers it will greatly increase your chances of hanging on to the customers you have already attracted. They'll come to view your business as useful to their lives, an integral part of their social scene.

If your business can create and curate relevant and valuable content across a range of digital platforms you will be in a much stronger position to affect and enhance the behaviour of your consumers. Just think how powerful celebrity Twitter accounts have become – a top name like Justin Bieber, Katy Perry or Barack Obama is in a phenomenally powerful position if they chose to use it as such. Think what a simple product endorsement on one of those accounts could achieve.

Now, I wouldn't suggest you get the President of the United States to tweet about your business, but I'm sure you get the point. This is an ongoing process that is about audience building rather than hard sales. It makes you the owner of your own media, rather than the person who buys space in a newspaper or TV or on radio to advertise your goods. In some ways, this new approach to selling is the art of communicating with your customers and prospects without actually selling.

It's constant. So instead of pitching products and services you post a steady stream of information that gives something to your prospective buyer – it could be knowledge, entertainment, new information or simply a great photo. If your business delivers consistent, ongoing valuable information to buyers, they will ultimately reward the effort and buy from you on a regular basis.

Like that!

THREE TOP TIPS

DO
Stick to what you know. You'll be able to grow quicker and provide a better service.

A PITFALL
You're not trying to take over the world (yet) so stay within your budgets and be careful not to get into any debt at this early stage of your business.

DON'T
Spend lots of money on advertising. Find out what customers you can attract organically first.

Chapter 4: Build Your Foundations

In this chapter:

- **How to make sure your business is ready to go**

- **Setting up bank accounts, PayPal, Amazon, eBay accounts – channel unity**

- **Introduction to business practice basics – accounts, pay etc**

Now, this is where I am going to have to contradict myself completely. For all that's good about planning, being sure of yourself and getting everything just right, if you wait for the right time to launch your business, you'll be waiting a very long time indeed. In fact, you'll probably be waiting forever. The truth is it's never the perfect time to start a business so get it started now! Stop planning, stop thinking and just get on with it.

I'm sure you're aware that most businesses fail, right? Well, actually most businesses don't even get started! The world is full of people asking 'what if' and lamenting 'if only' – so don't be another one of those people and *do something*. Now!

Running a business is like learning to ride a bike – at some point you're going to have to take those stabilisers off and just get pedaling (or peddling, of course, depending on what your business is!). But it's not until you feel the wheels turning beneath you that you actually realise what you really have to do to make it work. Once you're up and running you can see what needs to be done and work out how you're going to do it. And believe me, your legs are going to be going ten to the dozen for the first 18 months.

It's really important to remember that in the early stages, you will encounter all kinds of problems and be confronted by a seemingly endless series of hurdles. I'm not telling you this to put you off, only to open your eyes to the reality of running your own business. There's no point pretending otherwise, but there will be days when you will feel like quitting. You'll probably have quite a few days like that, but it's very normal, everyone goes through exactly the same problems. Just keep reminding yourself that it's all part of the journey and, almost certainly, working for yourself is much better than working for someone else.

Every now and then I take a moment to look back to 2008 when our business was just getting started. I can still see all the highs and lows and remember vividly how, at that time, every low felt like it was the end of the business. But we got through each one and now I see that some of our biggest growth spurts came immediately after hitting a low point.

Remember the whole Amazon scenario I mentioned earlier? That drove us to be more efficient and our sales grew rapidly because of that. Would we have made the changes we did if we hadn't had those problems? We'll never know, but I'm not so sure we would. The point is that you should greet every problem as a positive, an opportunity to learn something new about your business and a chance to improve. You have to know that dealing with a problem will make you a better person and enable you to make your business more efficient and effective.

And the challenges never stop coming. The key to overcoming obstacles is to embrace them, be glad they're in your way and recognise that you actually need them if your business is to keep growing. It's a bit of a cliché, but like many clichés, I find it to be very true – if you're finding the going easy, check that you're not going downhill.

We've established that if you're going to start your own business it is important to start it, but don't mistake spending lots of money for starting a business. Of course, there are costs involved in getting going – lots of costs in fact – but there are sharks in every stretch of water and there's a whole industry that has sprung up around starting businesses. It's easy to get carried away when you are launching a business and everyone has got advice for you, invariably for a price, but you don't need half the crap that people are going to try to sell to you. Saying 'no' is not as easy as you might think so practice it as often as possible.

However, you have to protect yourself against the things that can go wrong. Insurance is a must not least because there are various legal obligations you have to fulfill when employing people or selling products.

You'll most likely need:

- Employers liability insurance: This will help you compensate an employee who is injured or becomes sick as a result of the work they do for you. As soon as you become an employer you must get employers liability insurance worth at least £5 million and display your EL certificate in the workplace.

- Product liability insurance: This covers you against the cost of compensating anyone who is injured or made ill by a faulty product designed, made or supplied by your business. That also products your business includes repairs, refurbishes or remodels. Most businesses take out policies that cover them for claims of up to £5 million.

- Public liability insurance: This will cover you for claims made by members of the public for injury or damage to property in connection with your business and is designed to compensate for loss of earnings and any damages awarded, as well as legal costs. Some customers and clients will not work with your business unless you have public liability insurance.

Beyond that, you may well have equipment and stock, not to mention buildings and premises that also need insuring. It's a lot to take in, in one go, but don't let it put you off, shop around for a good broker and get it sorted. If you're a member of the Federation of Small Businesses (FSB), they can point you in the right direction and even provide discounts.

A few years ago we moved into a bigger warehouse. It was the middle of summer and things were going well. It was a new building with big metal secure doors and it meant we now had nearly 4000 sq ft of space in which to house all our stock and offices. I arranged and paid for all our insurance and booked the alarm fitters to come out. Although they couldn't get to us for just over a week I didn't think it would be a problem, they'd get to us when they could and everything would be OK. And then it happened.

What happened? The worst happened, that's what...

I got a phone call from a neighbouring business saying we had been broken into. Oh no! I was horrified. I drove to the warehouse to find one of the doors had been busted off and stock was strewn everywhere. The scumbags got away with stock worth about £5,000. Bastards!

The police were called in, prints were taken and I got a crime number. Then I called the insurance company. That's when things went from bad to worse. The alarm hadn't been fitted even though I had arranged for the job to be done. So, because the premises were not alarmed, the insurance policy wasn't valid and the stock wasn't covered. The insurance company wouldn't pay out because our alarm hadn't been fitted so the business had to take the hit and all because of a few days' gap before the alarms could be fitted. That was an expensive lesson to learn and a hard way to learn it. No matter how much you may think something like that won't happen to you I'm living proof that it can happen. And does. You must always protect yourself and your business.

While we're on about insurance here's another tip I wish I'd known about before I needed to – if you're going to be posting products to the USA and Canada, you'll need to mention this to your insurers as cover is not included as standard. The price depends very much on the size of your business and the goods you're posting, but if you're starting out fairly small, you should be able to get full cover for around £300.

Insurance is there to guard you and your business against the unexpected. Another form of protection – and one that's much cheaper – is good, old-fashioned customer service. If you take the time to find out exactly what your customers want, why they want it and what they're going to do with it, you can save them and you a great deal of time and hassle. It's incredibly important to make sure you're ready to deal with any customer queries as they come in. Don't keep people waiting they don't like it. If they do have to wait because you're busy, then tell them. Acknowledge their presence, let them know you realise they're waiting and get to them as soon as you can.

The same is true, perhaps even more so, if the query has come in by email. Set up a responder and use it whenever the email is unmanned, say you'll reply as soon as you can and then *make sure you do*! It's very easy for feedback and reviews to be left all over the internet these days, so you don't want to be upsetting your customers before you've even been able to serve them.

As a business owner, particularly a new business owner, you should deal with any complaints and observations from upset customers yourself as you are best placed to make fast and efficient decisions that will hopefully put things right. Things are a bit more difficult when it comes to the phone – do you have a call waiting system on hold, or do you use an answering machine? A lot will depend on your type of business and when the phones are unmanned. If it's for out of hours calls then use an answering machine with a message that reminds callers of your opening hours and directs them to the email address before giving them the opportunity to leave a message. If they do leave a message, *make sure you answer it.*

Don't use any of the remote receptionist, virtual office or call fielding services that are out there. Some businesses subscribe to them so that calls are always answered and because they think they create the illusion of a bigger business at work. They don't. It's always obvious that the call has been answered by an outside agency and it'll only serve to annoy your customers even more.

Here are some operations you need to be aware of in order to sell your products online.

PayPal

You'll need to open a PayPal account. PayPal is a company that manages online payments from buyers and passes the funds through to you. It takes a commission of 3.4% + 20p per transaction. This is their standard rate. The lowest rate available is 1.4% BUT and it's a big BUT you must apply for these lower rates. The actual rate you get is based on the volume of your sales so when you're starting out you should budget for the higher rate of 3.4% + 20p per transaction.
There are other ways that PayPal processes payments for you, which will have different charges. Your best bet is to phone PayPal and have a chat about your business and what you want to use the service for. You'll find the PayPal people are a very helpful bunch, contrary to popular belief.

With something like 150 million active PayPal users there's a lot of customers wanting to spend their money with you. However, there are other payment gateways such as Sagepay, Worldpay and Nochex, but PayPal is by far the market leader and is a payment option you simply have to offer on your website.

But as with any service there are some negatives. My biggest issue with PayPal is chargebacks. This is basically where a buyer makes a purchase from you then you get a message a few weeks later saying that the genuine cardholder is disputing the transaction. PayPal will put those funds on hold and ask for various bits of information from you. In my experience you will generally lose a chargeback case, so the money goes back to the cardholder and PayPal charges you a fee of £14.

This happens with most payment gateways. Online card fraud is a problem that you can limit but you'll never avoid it completely. We'll go into ways you can protect yourself a bit later.

When setting up your PayPal account, use an email address that is related to your business and make sure it is in keeping with your business. Having an address like sexy_pete69@hotmail.com might be appropriate in some business circumstances but not many. Buyers get to see this email address so keep it professional, or at least something inoffensive.

Your PayPal account will allow you to send and receive money, not only process sales. You'll be able to download all kinds of reports from PayPal to help with accounting and financial analysis. By far the best aspect of using PayPal though is the speed with which you'll be able to access your funds. Usually, once you request to withdraw the funds from your PayPal account, the money should hit your bank account if not immediately then certainly within a couple of hours. Some other processors can take as long as 15 days, so choose wisely.

Channel Unity

Finding a supplier and getting your products on your website is one thing, but you'll also need to be able to get those product details out in front of as many people as possible. This is where a company called Channel Unity comes in very useful.

Channel Unity acts as a gateway between your website and the various marketplaces out there such as Amazon and eBay. Basically, Channel Unity connects to your website and lists your products for sale on the various marketplace websites. Any changes you make to your product are also applied to the listing on the marketplace.
Through using Channel Unity we were able to add more than £300,000 to our turnover within a very short space of time. You pay Channel Unity a small fee of £15 per month plus 1% commission on your sales. Trust me, you need to sign up with this company. We have saved literally months of development time because their systems automate a lot of the hard work. If your database of products is fairly simple, you could be selling on up to 10 new marketplaces virtually overnight, certainly within a week.

We started using Channel Unity a couple of years ago and I was concerned that they may not be able to do what they said they could. So many companies talk a load of rubbish, just to get your money. But it was immediately obvious that we had found a great partner. It really does take a lot of the hard work off your hands and I can't praise the company enough. If you're serious about selling online, you have to register with Channel Unity.

Being involved in ecommerce has allowed me many freedoms that I would otherwise not be able to enjoy. Just this weekend I was out in Poole Harbour on my new boat, a Beneteau Antares 7.8. The sun was shining, the water was blue and some of the best scenery on the south coast was right there in front of me. I'm ever thankful for the life that selling online has given me and my family. It hasn't always been easy and the hard work never really stops, but you get to play harder too, which makes it much easier to deal with. Don't let anyone ever make you believe that you can't achieve the goals you have in your life. Keep pushing and keep fighting, you will make it.

When we started selling online, I remember thinking that we would need an accountant because I didn't know the first thing about business accounting. My focus was to sell as much as possible as fast as possible and we'll worry about the details later. Jeff Bezos, the CEO and founder of Amazon, is famous for his mantra, Get Big Fast. I absolutely believe he is 100% correct. Work out your profit margins and get selling – sell, sell, sell. In the early days nothing else matters. You want to build your customer base as fast as possible. Don't even worry too much about your profits, just focus on growth.

One piece of advice I hope you'll take is to hold off on employing people for as long as you possibly can. There

is nothing that costs a business as much as wages and employing people will eat up your cash faster than you can imagine. Even if you have to work 20 hours a day, seven days a week, do it. Only employ people once you have exhausted not only yourself but also all other options.
We have a great team now and we wouldn't be where we are without them, but in the early days, *do everything yourself.*

THREE TOP TIPS

DO
Realise that you're going to come up against many problems. These are not barriers to your success, these are lessons you must learn so that your business is strong enough to keep going.

A PITFALL
It's easy to assume you know how your customers feel about your business. But unless you ask them, how will you know? Seek their feedback and act on what they say.

DON'T
Take on staff until it is absolutely necessary. Wages are very expensive and will drain your cash flow more than anything else.

Chapter 5: Get Online

In this chapter:

- **How to get your products online and into all the marketplaces quickly and effectively**

- **Deciding how each product is represented, what to do about imagery and descriptions**

- **Building your own profile online**

So you've decided what you're going to sell, you've found your suppliers and you've set up all your accounts for PayPal, Amazon, eBay, Facebook, Twitter and YouTube. Good work. Now the real work can begin. This is where you actually put stock on the virtual shelves; show what you've got; display your wares. Napoleon said we are a nation of shopkeepers and he may have been on to something because it's as true today in the 21st century as it was back in the day.

In those days of course you had to have a shop on a busy street, you had to do it up, make it right, fix shelves to the walls and get plenty of change. Getting your products in front of the buying public is much simpler nowadays. In fact it's easy, once you know a few shortcuts.

Obviously you're online so you need to be thinking like an internet user as well as a seller. What do people search for? What kind of words do they put in to Google? How do they frame their searches? You'll need to make sure that when you give your products titles and names you take into account what people are going to be searching for, not necessarily what the manufacturer has called them. It might be a time consuming task to change all your product names, but it will be one of the best things you can do to make your business stand out.

Search Engines

Forget what you hear about Google's power being on the wane, it's rubbish. Google is still the world's number one search engine by far. More than 80% of individual internet users browse the web through Google, that's more than 110 billion searches every single day. The numbers are nothing short of phenomenal.

So most shoppers will bring up Google and tap in a search for the product they need. Google will then present what it thinks the person wants to see. However, these results can include other items, some of which you can also get your products to show up in. For example, if your items are also listed on Play.com, they submit your Play shop listings to Google so that they appear on the shopping pages within Google. This is all done automatically by Play. The same applies to eBay and other online sellers so the more you can get your items to stand out the better because by far the majority of your sales will, in one way or another, come through Google.

There are literally thousands of books and many millions of words out there telling you how to use Google, what you should and shouldn't do, when to do it, why you're doing it and so on. But it really doesn't need to be as complicated as that.

In a nutshell, Google tries to present data that is relevant to the person searching. It's that easy to understand. Your job is to make it as easy as possible for Google to find and understand the data that relates to your products and match it to the search so that it can present it to the person searching. That's also pretty easy to understand, but you'll have to work at staying on top of it.

Google loves an update, it's hungry for new data and unique content. Feed it new stuff and it will notice you more quickly and bump your products up the search rankings. It's down to you to keep your website bang up to date, checking it every day and making sure all the information is correct and every product is available to order. You've got to be on your A-game all the time with Google.

Luckily, Google provides you with a few ways to make all this quite easy. You can manage this yourself so there's no need to outsource the service and pay someone else a small fortune for doing it. Take the time to learn it yourself and make it part of your daily routine so that you know your site is always updated.

Here are some areas you'll want to research – spend a day online and you'll have this nailed:

Product Shopping Feed

A Product Shopping Feed is a list of products and their associated attributes, such as availability, condition, price, colour etc, that allows Google to present your products when users perform searches that match. You can get various pre-built modules that plug in to your website and automatically create these files and upload them to Google so your job is to make sure this file is kept up to date, providing Google with an update at least once a day.

There are various ways to create this file but in general it's no more complicated than using Excel or a similar spreadsheet program. Once you have created and uploaded your Product Shopping Feed, you'll want to back it up by activating some targeted adverts.

Product Listing Ads

These are similar to Adwords and if you're familiar with those little beauties you'll find it very easy to understand Product Listing Ads. The main difference is that a Product Listing Ad displays more information such as an image, seller information and product price. You will have to pay for them, but in my experience the conversion rates are very high. Switch on Product Listing Ads and get them right and you'll be getting sales immediately.

Companies can and do charge upwards of £500 a month to manage your Google Ad account, but as with most aspects of trading online, there are many thousands of videos available on sites like YouTube in which community-minded frequent users – in other words the day-to-day experts – show you how things work. You'll save a fortune by spending an hour or so teaching yourself to manage factors such as Product Listing Ads, Adwords and Product Shopping Feeds.

The vast majority of your website traffic and online sales will come through Google, but you'd be foolish to underestimate the reach of other search engines, particularly Yahoo, Ask, Bing and Duck Duck Go. Many will have similar features to Google, allowing you to advertise your products and services. Some offer services cheaper than others, but they all work so try them all. It's worth knowing though that what works well for one product type on one search engine may not necessarily work at all on another and each of the big search engines have quite specific demographics. I would recommend a trial of three months on each, which should give you enough data to see if that particular search engine works for you or not. Personally I would rank the top three search engines, in terms of their ability to generate sales for you like this:

- Google
- Bing
- Yahoo

Focus most of your efforts (and budget) on these and you won't go far wrong. There are always vouchers available, allowing you to try them for free in many cases. Computer magazines are a good place to find these, but a quick search and you should be able to track down a freebie offer or two. For example, Google are always giving away £75 Adwords vouchers and that £75 spent well can generate hundreds of pounds worth of sales.

You can now phone up Google on 0800-026-1700 and discuss your needs. They're really helpful and will make sure you get your account sorted as quickly as possible. It's worth doing because the reality is your business will struggle if you don't get this right as early as possible.

eBay

eBay is a marketplace that you'll want to get on. More than 17 million people log on to eBay every month, including 190,000 businesses and the site accounts for around 15% of the UK's total online shopping visits. It's easy and free to register, but then the hard work starts.

With eBay you'll be registered as a business seller and you'll be allocated a selling allowance. I'm not sure how they come to a specific number, but for a new trader it'll most likely be between £100 and £500 to start with. I think at the start we were limited to £150 a month.

You then have to contact eBay each month and ask to increase this allowance. Their decision is based on your sell through rate, that's the number of items you sell against the number of items you list. The higher your sell through rate the better chance you have of being able to increase your monthly selling allowance. It's quite a long process and it'll take six to eight months of constantly asking for increases for you to reach a decent amount.

Feedback will be your biggest challenge when dealing with eBay sales. People are very quick to leave negative feedback, particularly if delivery is late or if, in their opinion, the item isn't what they thought they had purchased. Feedback stings, not because it insults your business or is aimed at you personally, but because potential customers read feedback and make decisions based on what other people have said. They don't know the context of those comments, they don't know anything about the person that left them, all they know is what they read and because they read in on a website they trust, they believe it.

The point here is one that I can't stress forcefully enough. It is absolutely essential to have completely accurate product titles, comprehensive descriptions and clear images of all your products. Do it yourself by all means, but there's no shame in seeking professional help at this point and getting a copywriter and/or photographer in to give you the best chance possible. Spend time and, if necessary, splash the cash and get these things right and it will save you a lot of hassle later on, believe me.

Here's another thing eBay won't tell you, but it is vital you know it. If you have a personal account, selling stuff on eBay, close it. You cannot (safely) have a personal account and a business account on eBay not least because your personal account will attract higher rates of poor feedback amongst a host of other issues. No matter how hard you try it just will, so accept it and shut down your personal account because once your personal account has a few issues, eBay will start looking at your business account and before you know it, you're suspended from selling. That's that. Finito. No sales, no revenue, no income. What's more you will not be able to discuss this with anyone at eBay, you just hit a brick wall. Google is full of horror stories relating to this kind of behaviour by eBay, do a quick search, it makes for interesting reading.

That's a real horror story and no mistake. It can totally derail months of hard work and take even longer to put right again. However, it is an extreme.

One of the best things about eBay is that generally you'll receive all your payments via PayPal, which means you should have pretty much instant access to your money. Sometimes eBay will put a short temporary hold on the payment, especially for new sellers, to protect the buyer and you from any dodgy dealings.

I could write a whole book on eBay and how to trade on there but that's been done hundreds of times, but here are the main points you should remember when dealing on eBay:

Be honest

This might come as a surprise to you because it definitely did to me, but eBay buyers are completely different from buyers on your website. It's a total mystery why that should be, but they are. How are they different? Well, they are difficult to please, very touchy about descriptions and very quick to point out your shortcomings, this will help to make sure you get things right though.

All customers are precious, but you will find you need to work much harder at keeping eBay customers happy. You must be completely honest with your product descriptions, very precise and offer as many images as it takes to show the product exactly as it is. Do not gloss over anything.

However, get it right and eBay customers will reward you with positive messages.

Keep all this in mind when messaging them and speaking with them, always be ready to go the extra mile (actually that's true of all customers not just those on eBay), it will pay dividends in the end.

Feedback

It's the easiest thing in the world to get bad feedback. That package that was meant to go in Friday's post, but you left because you were in a hurry and now it won't go until Monday – that's bad feedback waiting to happen right there. A damaged box, grubby goods, scratches, faded colours, slightly different dimensions to those in your product description – all of it a ticking time bomb of bad feedback waiting to go off and damage your business.

Sometimes there are legitimate reasons for things not happening as they should. Sometimes the bad feedback is completely unwarranted and unfounded, it can even be downright malicious and spiteful. It is possible get bad feedback removed under certain circumstances, but you should do everything possible to not get it in the first place.

All sellers say feedback is important to them, but make sure you really mean it and always make the buyer aware how important it is to you. If possible when a customer takes the time and trouble to contact you about a sale, make sure you take the time and trouble to call them back. Don't hide behind emails and messages, it's impersonal and some might see it as rude. Once the buyer speaks to you and realises you're just a normal person, they're more likely to be fair with you.

Play by the rules

Familiarise yourself with eBay's rules, there enough of them! In fairness most of them are in place to protect you and your business as well as the sellers and not forgetting eBay's reputation and business as well.

A minor transgression of the rules could get your wrist slapped, but a major violation will get you booted off eBay for good.

Never rely on the income you get from eBay

Trading on eBay is essential but it is also unpredictable. There are all sorts of rules, regulations, checks and balances in operation and the truth is you might be acting in the best of faith but suddenly find yourself suspended from trading for some transgression of a rule you knew nothing about.

The simple fact is, any income from eBay can be taken away from you overnight and there will be little you can do about it. Treat eBay income as a bonus while it's there and try not to rely on it for paying your own bills.

Price matters

You'll quickly find that price is very important on eBay. It's very easy for people to compare prices and unless you're virtually the cheapest, you'll struggle to sell large quantities.

However, you can offset being slightly more expensive than your competitors if you can offer free delivery and prompt shipping. After price, those are the most important factors as far as eBay customers are concerned Get those right and you're on your way to having a successful eBay business.

I've been selling on eBay for many years. In the early days traders were encouraged to bid on their own auction items in order to bump the price up. Nowadays of course, doing this will quickly get you banned for good. Similarly, you used to be able to leave feedback for anyone, without even buying something, but that's no longer the case.

We've had all kinds of problems with eBay, but it remains a valuable and crucial source of revenue so we've worked hard to keep the right side of the eBay law enforcers.

We sell a lot of fancy dress and I've lost count of the number of times eBay have warned us for selling swords, even though we've explained they are plastic pirate toy swords. The listing gets pulled, we get warned, we explain what it is (again!), eBay apologise and we're allowed to relist it… only to have the same problem a few months later. It would drive us mad if we let it.

Once we had an eBay account, established for more than three years, with at least 40,000 feedback. I woke up one day and it was gone, suspended for breaching some rule, which they never did elaborate on. We appealed for weeks, going from department to department but with no luck. No-one at eBay would or could explain why the account was gone, but it had been ended and that was that.

It was one of those times I've mentioned before, when you have to look at your business and quickly adapt. That account would typically bring us in around £50,000 for a Halloween season, so we had to find a way to replace that income. This is why I say don't rely on eBay, it can be taken away from you in the blink of an eye.

We're back on eBay now and have been for many years, competition is very tough and it's harder to make money on there than ever, but get it right and have some unique products and it's more than possible to make a good living from it. It's just much harder work than other online selling platforms.

Amazon

Amazon is the golden egg of ecommerce. I cannot stress highly enough the importance of selling on Amazon. Around half of our turnover comes from Amazon and it's instant. You can list as many items as you like, no limits like on eBay, you can be up and running in an afternoon, with sales coming in immediately.

Amazon has websites in many countries around the world. For us, the best ones are the UK, Germany and France. Spain and Italy have a few problems with sales being relatively low and USA is quite hard to compete on due to the extra costs of shipping from the UK, but that will depend on what you're selling.

Amazon pays out on your sales every two weeks, direct into your bank account, deducting their fees, which are around 17%. This is quite a large chunk, but the sales volumes you'll be able to hit will go a long way to offsetting those fees. The reporting tools they have that allow you to track sales and returns are not only extremely useful, they're also very easy to use.

The key to being successful on Amazon is getting the 'buy' box - the little blue box on the right-hand side of the page with the 'Add to Cart' button. Amazon don't tell you exactly how to get the 'buy' box, but as long as your price is competitive, your feedback is good and the various other statistics they monitor are all kept under control, you shouldn't have too much trouble getting it right.

Remember this – excellent customer service is key with Amazon.

Managing your sales sites

Once you've got your website and all your other selling accounts set up, you'll need a way to manage them as easily as possible. I now use Channel Unity. What they do is take all your products on your website and list them onto the various marketplaces. Then when you sell something on Amazon for example, the Channel Unity system passes that order back down the chain and onto your website. This enables you to manage your orders in one place.

It's great because it also takes any updates you do to products on your site, such as prices, descriptions and images, and updates those products on eBay and Amazon as well. This will save you literally hours of work.

I'm really trying to avoid telling you how to do all the tasks needed as I feel it is really important that you go through that learning curve yourself. It's not the only way of learning something, but doing it yourself is often the best way. But a few pointers along the way never did anyone any harm and I'm looking to just point you in the direction of things and systems that have worked for us, in the knowledge that they can work for you too. It took us years to discover these things, there's no need for it to take you as long.

Nobody sells anything for you for free though so as far as income from trading on these various sources is concerned, your ultimate goal is for the majority of sales to come through your website. That's where customers will see the real you, that's the online space you have complete control over. Selling through your own site means you won't have to pay the extra fees that you do on the other sites and it helps your brand as customers get to know the real you.

Social Media

Social media is something that's become such an integral part of business life these days, that if you're not taking part, you're missing out on a lot of potential customers.

Twitter is all about engagement. It's a way you can instantly communicate with people, many of whom are your customers or potential clients. It's also very effective. Sometimes a customer will take a look at your social media presence, to see how you come across – are you helpful, are you consistent, or worse, are you invisible?

If you're going to do Twitter and Facebook, you have to keep it fresh and you have to do it whole heartedly. There's no room for half-arsed attempts with this, your customers will simply walk away.

Besides, Twitter and Facebook can be great fun and there's no better way to get closer to your customers. Don't be afraid of showing your own face and don't hide behind your company name. People love people, so get your name out there – and that means you, not your business. Show the public what you're all about, be honest and they will appreciate it.

The big corporate companies really lose out when it comes to personality. Why do you think Sir Richard Branson is always in the public eye? He's the face of Virgin and the people love it, they can connect with him. He writes his own blog, tweets regularly and connects with staff and customers very directly. More than anything, he is the personality of Virgin, the thing people relate to when they think of the brand.

Buyers will often do some research on your company before buying from you. This gives you the perfect chance to show them how great you are. First thing, I would advise is to set up all the social media channels. Register them in your company name if they're still available now in case someone else does. Only use them for business related news, but keep it personable – this is not the place for corporate talk. Keep it fun and current and respond to any queries promptly.

Success is a strange word when you really think about it. When I was younger and struggling to make ends meet, success for me was getting a job. Simple as that.

Now it's selling over a million pounds' worth of stock. I wouldn't have dreamed that I could ever be in this position, but am forever thankful that I am.

One of the most difficult things I found was letting go of caring what people think. I don't mean that you shouldn't be considerate of those around you, more that people will say many things, not always for the reasons you might think. Everyone has an agenda; their agenda. Ultimately there are very few people in this world whose prime concern is you, there are some but very few. You have to look out for yourself so when those around you are giving you their advice, listen… but with only one ear! You do it your way, right?

We're told throughout most of our life that we should go to school, pass our exams, get a job, find a partner, have kids, get a pension, get old and die. Says who? I mean, who makes this stuff up? You do what's best for you and your family and screw what everyone else thinks. It's never too late to be the person you've always wanted to be. I drifted for years, never knowing what direction I should be going in, but the lessons I learned along the way have served me well in my business endeavours. I'm far from perfect, but believe me, you don't need to be perfect.

THREE TOP TIPS

DO
Get all your products published onto the search engines via their various systems as fast as you can and keep them up to date.

A PITFALL
Watch how much you spend on advertising your products via the search engines. You'll often be paying for each click and those clicks soon add up. Start slow and then up your spend as you understand the system more and have ironed out the creases. Also, don't put all your eggs in one basket. It's all too easy to rely on one marketplace for all your sales, spread it round.

DON'T
Don't copy what other people are doing. What works for them may not work for you. It depends heavily on individual factors such as product type, price, location. Never use stock images and descriptions if you can help it. Having bespoke information will help your rankings on the search engines.

Chapter 6: Gain Market Share

In this chapter:

- **How to get your customers to notice you**

- **How to get your customers to buy from you**

- **How to get your competitors' customers to buy from you**

Getting noticed online is where the hard work really starts. No matter how fancy your website is or how great your prices or products are, if no-one knows about you, there's no point, it will have all been for nothing. The internet is a marvelous thing, it's hard to imagine a life without it, and almost half the world's population has an internet access – that's a vast customer base of around 2.7 billion people – but if you're going to make your business work, they've got to know about you, or be able to easily find out about you.

There are some basic things you should be doing at this point. You'll have your social media accounts set up on Facebook, Twitter, Instagram and YouTube. They're great and they will drive some traffic to your website, but not enough to survive. You'll also have your products listed on Google. Again, this is just as it should be and it will give you some sales, but not enough to get by.

You'll also need to get a bit old school and put yourself about.

Depending on what you're selling, you have various options open to you. For example, if you're selling funny suits, dress up in one with a bunch of your friends and get out there on the high street. Make a fool of yourself, have a laugh, make other people laugh – it's fun and it's free and it will generate some local interest. Invite the local paper along, play up to the cameras, get noticed – the story will give you something to share on your Facebook page and Twitter feed.

There's no shortage of self-styled publicity gurus who'll promise you the moon on a stick in return for a tasty monthly retainer, but be careful. Before you pay anyone to promote your business, ask yourself this question: would I get more publicity if I simply threw the £2000 fee up in the air in the middle of town?

A lot of these PR agencies will take your money, post a few ads online and laugh themselves silly at their next boozy, schmoozy lunch. As a general rule of thumb, anyone who is really good will come to you through a recommendation, they'll have a proven track record, understand the needs of a growing business and be packing a contacts book loaded with names at local newspapers, magazines, radio and television – the kind of people that can make things happen.

So before you go throwing money away, let's get you started on the right track. You'll already have checked out your competition, but take a closer look at what they're doing, see what works for them, work out how it can work for you – and do it better. It's that simple. That one thing will get you more traction than anything else in the early days. You're taking all the lessons your competitors have learned and applying them to your business in one hit. Don't worry about people thinking you're copying them, just do it. After all, they say imitation is the sincerest form of flattery!

It's exactly what we did when we launched our magic business. I took all the lessons we had learned in our first business then looked at what the other magic companies were doing. I kept all the things I knew were good and simply applied them to the new business. Within six months we were turning over in excess of £250,000. We became one of the largest magic companies in the UK before we were even a year old.

When you enter a new market and start rocking the boat with your new ideas, you'll most likely attract the attention of others in that market – the competition. They'll email you telling you that your prices are too cheap, or advise you that what you're doing isn't the way things are done. Ignore every single word. They're scared – and so they should be – because you're taking market share from them.

The thing is they probably started their own business in the same way and now they're worried you'll come along and upset the apple cart. Tough. It's business and you've got a living to earn.

When we started our fancy dress company back in 2007, we often received emails and messages from our competitors. At first we were a bit surprised, but we've got thick skins so we ignored them. However, others might find it a little intimidating. They would tell us that we were too cheap and that we should put our prices up. Then there'd be a whole load of stuff about how they had been in the business for years and how the internet was going to ruin the whole industry for everyone.

You what?

It soon dawned on me that what they actually meant was that they didn't have the ability, know-how, energy or imagination to adapt their business to succeed online. So, rather than get with it and buck their ideas up, they obviously decided to spend all their time and energy trying to put everyone else off.

Needless to say they are now out of business.

Once you start spending more time on attacking your competitors than you do on running your own business, the end is nigh. Of course, you should know what other people in your sector are doing and you'll find it pays to take the trouble to find out, but you should only use that knowledge to improve your own business.

It's war out there you know!

This is where you need to get involved with what's going on within your chosen industry. You need to sign up for all your competitors' newsletters, like their Facebook pages and follow them on Twitter. You want to make sure you know as much about them as they know about themselves. That way you'll be able to see what it is they're doing that is attracting buyers.

If your competitors are getting a sale out of doing something, do it yourself. Copy everything they do that helps them get sales, so long as it's legal of course!

Why do you think they're doing it? Because it works, that's why. And how did they start doing it? They copied someone else of course.

It's a good time to learn that it's not all about price either. You won't get more sales simply by being the cheapest. It doesn't work like that. Price is not the main factor that makes people decide to buy. In fact, some of the most important factors are trust, the cost of shipping and being able to return an item should there be a problem. The typical buyer will weigh all these factors up and then apply the price factor.

For example, if you find a website selling Product A for £45 and another site selling the same thing for £30, what's the first thing you think? Do you think the more expensive website is ripping you off by being overpriced; or do you think the cheaper website is going to rip you off once you make the purchase?

Either could be true, but in any case, my point is that you wouldn't just jump in and buy the cheaper one; you'd look at the other factors first.

So here are some things you can do to make it easier for potential customers to decide to buy from you:

- Make your delivery costs clear and easy to understand.

- Provide free shipping if possible.

- Make sure you follow any laws regarding returns and where possible allow free returns. Again, make sure your returns procedure is simple and the instructions are very easy to find on your website, not buried on a terms and conditions page.

- Put your actual address and contact numbers on your homepage, in the header ideally so that they are always visible.
You'd be surprised how many websites don't even do these few simple things. It doesn't take a lot to get them right, but take the trouble to do so because they work, trust me.

Once you've got people buying from you, the name of the game is to keep them coming back. You need to look after your customers as they are the most important asset of your business. Without them you're nothing and your business will fail. What you must be aiming for every day is to make your customers feel special. The customer that feels your love will remain loyal. Let them know how much you appreciate their custom and make sure you mean it because they can very easily go elsewhere.

I'm going to assume that anyone reading this is a good, honest, hard-working person, with impeccable morals and ethics. To be honest I've no evidence that you're anything but that and I prefer to think the best of people until proved otherwise, so why not?

Of course, if you are a good, honest, hard-working person with impeccable morals and ethics, you should make sure your customers know this about you. Trust is one of the main factors when buying from anyone online. If people trust you, they will buy from you. But the thing about trust is that you can't buy it, you can only earn it and once you've earned it you need to work hard to keep it because it's a hell of lot easier to lose.

No amount of fancy adverts or flash brochures will make people trust you. The only way to build trust with them is to get out there and build it. Be seen. Get your face up on your social media channels, publish a blog, preferably a video blog, or even write a book. Be seen in local media, sponsor a kids' sports team, or put your company name to a local award. Get your name and your business associated with good works and positive news. It's invaluable when it comes to building trust within the community. Anything that allows people to see your personality will help your business grow.

It's an example I come back to time and time again, but one person who is very good at this is Sir Richard Branson. Rarely does a company as big as Virgin command such respect from the general public. The fact that it does is down to one person and one person only – Sir Richard Branson. And you have to take your hat off to him. That part of his success is due entirely to the fact that he puts himself about, gets out there, he's not afraid to get down and dirty in the trenches. He'll set himself up for a fall, he'll speak up about issues that concern him and he'll take very public risks if he feels it is in his interests. Everyone loves Richard, right? And if you love Richard, you love Virgin.

Remember this – you are the Sir Richard Branson of your company, so get out there and do it. It's never too late to be the person you always wanted to be, all it takes is for you to decide to make it happen.

Every single day millions are spent online and it's your job to get your share of that money. But it's important to remember that you're also a customer so don't stop thinking like one. What would make you buy from you? If you stumbled upon your website today, is there anything that would put you off? Go and have a look right now and be brutally honest with yourself about it because in the early days your customers don't know you from anyone and, to be frank, they couldn't care less about you or your business. You need to be that harsh with yourself also.

Your biggest source of new customers is likely to be those of your competitors. That sounds tough, but think about it for a moment. It's obvious they want to buy the products and services you're selling as they already are, just not from you. Yet.

So how do you get them to try buying from you?

There are three very clear stages to this. First, you'll need to get them to notice you. Then you'll need to give them a reason to try you; and finally you'll need to make them want to come back to you.
Let's take each stage one at a time.

- How to get competitors' customers to notice you.

Making your competitors' customers aware of you is very different from general advertising. It's best if you take a very indirect approach. The problem is, if you just jump in their faces and say how wonderful you are and how rubbish your competitors are, you're actually criticising the very customers you're trying to win over. You're telling them they're not making very good choices and you're questioning their judgement. Nobody likes to be called a fool, least of all by someone they don't know. Although some of the supermarkets employ these overtly negative tactics in their advertising it's a very difficult approach to get right and will in all likelihood have the exact opposite effect to the one you set out to achieve.

It pays to be subtle. You want to help your competitors' customers stumble upon you, as if by accident. Make sure your website is in all the places your competitors advertise, blog about what your competitors are blogging about and promote the products they're promoting. This creates a feeling of familiarity among their customers, so that as they are drawn towards your business they'll see things they recognise and feel comfortable shopping with you.

I'm no psychologist, but there are all sorts of decisions and processes at play here. Ultimately your goal at this point is to not alienate anyone and to create an air of recognition.

- Give them a reason to try you.

Once these customers know about you, they'll be intrigued. However, their loyalty will still be with your competitor so you need to give them a reason to try your business. The best way to achieve this is to have a product in stock that the others don't. That way the buyer doesn't feel like they're breaking any loyalty towards your competitor.

Another way is by adding value, maybe giving a free gift with the first order placed with you, or free shipping on all orders this month. By adding something extra, you're giving them something in return for them buying from you. Play your cards right and it should be the start of a beautiful relationship.

- Make them want to come back.

When we post out our orders, we include a flyer with a 10% discount code. This entitles our customer to come back and get money off their next order. It gives the customer a reason to use us again and not to look elsewhere.

You're ultimately in business to make money, but there's no question about it, you have to give to get. You can't expect people to come along and buy stuff from you just because it's you. They don't know you. They couldn't really care about you in actual fact. What the customers are looking for are the deals, the free shipping offers, the vouchers, free gifts. Give them what they want and keep on giving them what they want and they are far more likely to reward you by becoming your loyal customer.

Making your buyers want to return is a great way of getting sales. Think about it, they have already spent money with you and received their goods, so the trust is there. Although gaining customers costs money in the short-term, offering a discount to a returning customer is the best way to keep that customer.

OK so you may have to take a 10% hit or so on the order, but you'll be saving money in the long run by not having to source new customers all the time. Your best asset will always be your existing customers so it's up to you to do what you have to do to keep them coming back at all costs.

If this all sounds like a blueprint for success it's because it is... provided everything goes to plan. The trouble is it's not an exact science and there are many random factors that can trip you up at every turn. You have to be prepared to think on your feet and react to changing circumstances it's part of what makes working for yourself such fun. I love it.

One thing I can just about guarantee for you though is that, no matter how well it goes, you will not be able to achieve massive gains within weeks. It takes months to get a foothold in your sector – maybe more depending on how much competition there is. That is why it is so important to keep things tight and pay attention to Google Analytics. Once you start to make sense of the information and realise that more and more people are visiting your website and buying from you, the next thing you'll need to do is target people that buy your goods/services, but from your competitors, and convert them to your business so they begin to buy from you.

Google Analytics plays a big part in keeping track of how your business is growing. You'll be able to see if the number of people visiting your site is increasing. If it is you'll be able to gauge how quickly your popularity is growing, which in turn will give you a good idea whether or not all that hard work is paying off. Once the number of people visiting your site starts to rise, you'll be able to get more accurate data on conversion rates, that is, the number of visitors that actually buy something.

You can look at a graph covering the last few months plotted against sales. You'll be hoping to see a rising trend, a steady increase in sales over time. Of course, many businesses are seasonal so you may see a spike or two along the way – a bank holiday weekend, seasonal celebrations like Christmas and Easter perhaps, or even a bout of really good weather, all of these can explain rapid increases in business.

Within your Analytics account you'll be able to mark certain points of interest on the timeline. So, for example, if you had a special sales event or promotion on your website, you can mark this so that you'll be able to see if the sale had any effect on sales or visitor numbers and so on.

If you can measure it, you can improve it. So measure everything.

Once you start winning market share from your competitors, you'll probably find that they'll start getting more aggressive in their techniques. The biggest mistake you can hope they make is for them to start cutting their prices. Honestly, I've seen it happen and when it does I'm a happy chappie. If the competition is cutting prices it means you've got them on the run. Slashing prices in an effort to get more customers only achieves one thing… cutting profits.

And if a business isn't making enough money, then it's only a matter of time before it will fail. If your competitors are dropping their prices it means you're winning market share and customers from them.

But I love competition. I love the contest, pitting my wits against those of a competitor. If anything it makes me a little sad when another business goes under because that's another player out of the game for the time being.

Competition is a great thing and without it the business world would be a very different and dark place.
What some people fail to realise though is that there are many, many different things we can choose to compete on. Obviously there's price, who can sell the cheapest or who can sell the most, but there's also quality of service, speed of delivery, different brands, availability of the product, choice of products, follow up service, reputation, the list goes on and on. You'd be well advised to avoid a price war if you can – just ask the supermarkets – it only ever hurts the businesses involved.

As I said before, the existing customer base is the biggest single asset of any business, particularly one that sells its wares online. Those customers can save you a small fortune in marketing costs as well.

What better reason to buy anything than on recommendation? Amazing as it may seem, but in this age of instant digital communication with our smartphones, emails and internet, old-fashioned word of mouth is still the holy grail of the retailer. Get someone to recommend your product and your business to their friends and you've got almost instant customer loyalty.

Along with getting your existing customers to continue buying from you, think about their friends. Give your valued customers a reason to introduce their friends to your business and the goods or services they've bought from you. A great way to do this is by offering them the chance to share their purchase on social media sites like Facebook. As your customers complete their checkout success, you can have a button that will instantly post a message on their social media pages showing their friends and followers what they've just bought and where they got it.

Further to that there's nothing wrong in offering your existing customers a discount if they bring a friend to your online store. Give them a code to pass on to their friends that will entitle the new customer to a special deal as well as secure money off for the existing customer on completion of their next order. It's easy to keep track of how many of these special codes are redeemed and the news that you are issuing them in the first place is ideal content for your own social media outlets to be liked and shared by your followers.

Word of mouth really is the ultimate referral. You can't beat it and you can't buy it, but you can make it easier for people to do it. Social media is becoming more and more relevant in online sales as it provides an instant way for people to share their thoughts and actions and can quickly generate extra sales, especially at key seasonal times of the year, when last minute sales make up a big part of your turnover.

Embrace social media, get to know how to get the most from it and, most importantly of all, have fun with it.

THREE TOP TIPS

DO
Get to know your competitors. Sign up to their newsletters and read them, follow them on social media and take note of what they're doing.

A PITFALL
Forgetting the basics is very easy. Make sure your customers can find your address and telephone number. This is not just good practice, but it is a legal requirement. Avoid websites that don't do this.

DON'T
Think that cutting your prices is the best way to get more customers, it isn't. Add value in other ways.

Chapter 7: It's Good To Talk

In this chapter:

- **Keeping customers by regular communication, emails, newsletters, offers, deals**

- **Maintaining the conversation over time**

- **Using your existing customer relations to attract new customers**

Getting people to buy from you is one thing, but making sure they come back and buy from you again is the key to creating and maintaining a successful business. If there was a formula for how to do that I'd be the wealthiest man in the world, but there's not. Having said that, it's not all down to luck either. You have to work very hard to win customers and even harder to keep them once you've got them.

This is where I want to share a few tips and ideas about how you look after the people that make your business what it is – your customers.

One of the biggest mistakes you can make is thinking you've cracked it the minute your sales start coming in. Getting the process right, making sure you provide great service and delivering the goods on time is great, but three months later when that same person needs your product or service again, will they remember you?

Without a bit of effort it's unlikely they will to be honest. So, how can you help that customer to think of you the next time they need you?

It helps if you view your customers as partners – they partner you in the transaction, you need them every bit as much as they need you, perhaps more so. Think of them as people you have to build a relationship with, communicate with regularly and be interested in. It's not all about offering them special deals, discounts and promotions either – too many of those can seriously undervalue your goods and services. Engage with them through social media, email them regularly with your business newsletter, invite their responses on Instagram and YouTube, find out what they're doing and what makes them tick, the things that interest them.

I'm not suggesting you stalk them or take them all out for drinks, but I'm sure you get the picture. I make no apology for returning to this time and time again, but your biggest asset is your existing customer base. They're the ones you know, or should do; they're the ones that have felt the benefit of your excellent service, great prices and top quality products before; they're the ones that shouldn't need convincing to shop with you again. You know who your existing customers are because you've got their contact details and you also know something about what they like because you know what they bought last time. That means these are by far the easiest customers to talk to.

People love to talk, especially about themselves and the things they've done. That's at least part of the reason why social media is so popular – it gives everyone a platform to share their thoughts and experiences and allows everyone else to see what they've been up to.

If you've got people talking then why not try to get them to talk to you, or about you? Join in the conversation, ask them questions, point them in the direction of new 3lines, show an interest in their lives and the things they do. It makes an impression on people and they'll be only too eager to tell their friends about it. Word of mouth has and always will be the best form of advertising because you can't buy it no matter how much money you've got – that's what makes it so valuable.

Get things wrong of course and that same word of mouth can come back and bite you hard. Very hard in fact, a bad reputation will bring you crashing down even faster than you think so keeping on top of issues and dealing with things efficiently, effectively and with the minimum of fuss is absolutely critical when it comes to building and maintaining great customer relations.

Your digital management system will most likely have a way of creating and sending newsletters by email. It should be possible to set up a few different eye-catching designs that can be targeted towards specific groups of recipients. For instance, you could have one design for customers that buy from you on a regular basis, another for customers that haven't purchased from you within the last three months and one for your new customers.

You could further break down your customer base into age, geography and even special interest groups. Use what you know about your customers intelligently and you could contact them before they even know they need you. As an example, if you know a customer has a stag or hen event planned it might be reasonable to think a year later they'll be planning a first wedding anniversary, or maybe there could be a new-born in the offing at some point. The information could be completely useless, but it might also tap into another source of revenue that you might otherwise not get.

The messages and offers you include in these various emails will obviously need to be very different so spend a bit of time considering what you want to say to each group and how you think it's best to say it. You know your customers better than anyone – or you should do – so you'll know the best way of communicating with them. If you're not sure of the exact words to use, or how to design the email, seek professional help. If you know what you want and can be clear about the brief it shouldn't cost you a fortune and will be money well spent when the orders start to roll in.

For example, an existing customer may be more interested in your newer products or an exclusive offer for their continued loyalty; whereas a new customer will be looking for a reason to make that initial purchase, so perhaps a free delivery option will work well. Ideally you want to take an order from each of them, but each will need a very different approach. It often depends on what you're selling and you may have to employ a few different tactics until you find one that works. The point here is not to treat all your customers as though their needs are identical because they're most definitely not.

Pricing is always a complex issue. You know the margin you need to see out of your products and you price them competitively so there probably isn't a great deal of room for discounting lines. Unless you want to work for nothing it will pay you to be very careful when offering discounts. There are people who will only buy when you have an offer or reduced prices, but this defeats the purpose of what you're trying to achieve, which is ultimately to make more money by getting more customers. It's far better – and by better I mean more profitable – to add value rather than cut prices. Making someone feel good about buying from you needn't cost you a penny. Reacting to their order promptly and efficiently, packing and shipping it properly, taking care to keep them informed about their order and dealing with any issues arising from the order with a good heart all add value to your service and can make a massive difference when a customer is weighing up who to buy from.

People really dislike paying for delivery, it's one of our biggest bugbears, so anything you can do to help your customers in this area will always be welcome. Free delivery on orders over a certain amount is an absolute must these days so invest a bit of time and work out what value to set to achieve free delivery by looking at your Google Analytics data. Adding value is not only cheaper for you, it helps to make your business stand out from the others. A good idea is to have one day a month where all orders over £10 qualify for free shipping for example. It gives people something to share and saves them a few quid.

There's a whole host of websites that specialise in offers and deals these days – it's got to the point where people seem to expect a discount just for asking – but as I've said, discounting your prices is a very dangerous thing to do and is a fast way to lose money. Offering a saving if someone shares your page on Facebook or Twitter is a growing trend and it works well as it's a great way to get your name out there. It's a form of word of mouth so give it a go to see if it works for you – it'll cost you less to offer those discounts than to pay an agency, so it's more of an investment on your part.

I've had the pleasure a few times of meeting with Mark Pearson, the founder of MyVoucherCodes.co.uk, which he recently sold for £55 million. His whole website is based on offering discounts for products and services and the site is the first port of call for many thousands of people trying to find a discount code before they go shopping to make their purchases.

It's a clever business model because MyVoucherCodes.co.uk collates all the special offers in one place so shoppers don't have to go searching all over the internet to find them. It attracts so many hits that companies want to be on the site, but to be on the site they have to offer discounts. That's great for the buyer, but not so good for the seller, as you'll never really know if you would have got the sale in the first place, without offering the discount.

The thing is because so many businesses are on these discount code websites, you're almost forced into joining them to make sure you don't miss out on additional sales and maybe some brand exposure. It made me think long and hard before committing, believe me.

It's down to what will work best for your business, but in the early days when you're trying to get your name out there, I would recommend you use these discount websites as there's no doubt about it, they do give you a traffic boost and a welcome extra few sales.

If nothing else it will give you something to tell your customers about in your next newsletter. It's important that once you start sending out emails and newsletters that you keep doing it. Your customers will quickly become accustomed to receiving information from you and it won't be long before they are actively looking forward to getting your messages. This is exciting. It means you are making a mark on people's lives and becoming part of their routine, something regular they have come to enjoy.

This kind of communication is a great way to build loyalty, as long as the content is what the customers want. Whatever you send has to be of use to the customer otherwise they'll start to think you're wasting their time with a load of useless information. If you're not sure, ask them, they'll soon tell you.

If your customers have signed up to receive your email updates, you should be looking to send an email every week, on a set day. The day and time you choose to send them is very important and can have a dramatic effect on the open rate and click-throughs – that's the number of people that click on a link in the email.

There have been many studies on the best time and day to do this, but it depends mainly on what you're selling and to whom. Try a few different days and times to find out the best times for you, experiment a bit. Start by sending on Monday lunchtime for example, then try 5pm on a Friday – go for extremes as they should provide the most markedly different results to compare. There are various pieces of software that can monitor the performance of newsletters, do a quick Google search for newsletter software and you'll soon find something you feel comfortable with.

There are some key times to avoid though, such as the weekend. It's almost pointless sending out emails so that they're waiting in the recipients' inboxes on a Monday morning. You know what it's like yourself. When you've not logged on for a day or so and your inbox is chock-a-block with emails it's inevitable that something will get missed, or deleted by accident, or left aside to look at later and forgotten.

It's all about getting noticed, but just as important is getting those that do notice you to do a little work for you – like forward your message to their friends. It's vital for your email to include a way for the recipient to easily send it on to their friends and contacts. A great big share button or something similar ought to do it, but you could just as easily offer an incentive for them to recommend their friends because, generally speaking, people will trust a friend's recommendation over any advert.

As I said before it's all about relationships and building a rapport with your customers is a vital part of growing your business, not only because happy customers spend more, but because your regular customers are a great source of feedback and feedback is the lifeblood of your business. For all the careful planning and meticulous execution, until you start something you can never know how it will work until you launch it.

If you're thinking of trying a new feature on your website for example, ask your existing customers for their opinion. What do they think of it? Is it a good idea? Will it improve their visit to your website? How would they do it? When should it start? There are dozens of questions to ask your customers and an almost infinite number of responses, but among them could be the nugget that makes the difference to your business. Your existing customers know a bit about your business through their dealings with it and are more likely to be honest with you. It might just save you spending time and money on features or services that may not be required.

Over time those existing customers will effectively become brand ambassadors for your company. They've found something they like – your business – and they naturally want to tell their friends about it. In fact, they'll actively enjoy nothing more than telling their peers what a great business it is, how good its products are, what wonderful service they get and all manner of good stuff. All of which is advertising you cannot buy – and great for future sales of course.

With the magic company I own, I often have magicians calling me up or sending emails, asking about our latest items and what I would recommend them to buy. Now, I've pulled the odd rabbit out of a hat as far as my business is concerned, but I'm not a professional magician by any stretch of the imagination. However, I love the fact professional magicians ask me to recommend products to them because it shows they trust me. When your customers trust you, it means all the hard work you've put in is really starting to pay off because trust is one of the biggest considerations for buyers when shopping online, especially these days with so many nightmare stories regarding identity theft and credit card fraud.

At the end of the day it's all about customer contact – the more you have the better. In this age of instant communication staying in touch with friends, family and, yes, customers has never been easier, but it amazes me just how wrong some companies can get it. I often browse through all kinds of Twitter accounts, looking for interesting snippets, or to see what people are talking about in my industry and it always surprises me the way some companies use social media in general. It's usually one of two things – either they only ever post about their own products/services and there's something from them 50 times a day; or their last post was three months ago.

If I see a social media account where the last post was longer than about a day ago, it makes me wonder why they can't find the time to spend 10 minutes a day talking to their customers. If they don't have the time to do that, will they have the time to treat me and my order correctly?

It's important to feel confident when you send your payment and personal details into the ether that your information is going to be respected, treated properly and looked after. If a company has gone to the trouble of setting up a social media presence and then can't be bothered to maintain it properly, I'm definitely going to be wondering what they'll do with all that valuable information about me.

The daft thing is, with just a little effort there are some fantastic ways to engage people through the various social media platforms. Twitter uses hash tags, a hash tag is this symbol: #. If I include the term #fancydress in my tweets, anyone searching for fancy dress related posts will find mine. Many TV shows use hash tags as a way their viewers can follow the show, access additional content, or tweet about the show with other viewers while watching.

Go on Twitter now and search for #worldcup or #art and you'll see better how it works. Now do some searches for terms related to your area of business, you're sure to find some interesting pieces of information. Facebook recently introduced hash tags, they work similarly to the way they work in Twitter.

On Facebook you should try to include photos in your posts, they get far more likes and comments than posts without photos and videos even more so. The good thing about Facebook is that you're able to make it much more personal, due to there being no limit to the number of characters you can use. Famously, Twitter has set a limit of 140 characters per tweet, although there's been a lot of debate recently and I expect they will raise that soon.

When you sit down to create your newsletters, try to remember that the reader will take less than three seconds to decide whether or not to open it or delete it. It's harsh, but all that effort you put into creating something that's eye catching and informative gets less than three seconds to make an impression on the recipient. That's why it is so important to know what gets people clicking.

Nothing arouses interest like a bit of mystery, a hint of the unknown. People are generally pretty curious, or maybe it's just that we're nosey, but make them want to know something and they'll be clicking for Britain. It's definitely a great way to get people clicking on links. For example, if you include some products that you're selling in your email, don't put the price on it, but do add a flash to highlight the percentage discount you're offering. Alternatively, give the recipient a very limited time period, even as little as a few hours, to grab the deal or whatever it is you're offering before it closes.

The point is that there must be a call to action; you must give the recipient a reason to take action. This is either a phrase or perhaps an image that tells the reader to do something and it could be as simple as 'Click here now' or a more subtle approach such as 'Only 3 left, don't miss out'. As with so much of this advice, it's never an exact science so it's back to trial and error – experiment with lots of different offers and try several calls to action to find out what works best and fits your brand.

It's not a time to be shy though, don't be afraid to be bold, you'll be surprised how many people want to be sold something. I take the view that if someone wants my money for their product, they are going to have to be prepared to sell it to me – and I know I'm not alone, many people are the same. Pitching products for sale through newsletters and emails is not just a case of slapping a picture of the product on a page with a price tag attached. You need to get creative. Try reviewing the products you sell and email your customers with those reviews. Better still, get your customers to write in with their reviews and use the best of those in your sales literature.

Other people, potential new customers, will want to hear from shoppers that have bought from you. They want to read real people's experiences, warts and all, as it reassures them that you're a genuine seller, so let your buyers voice their opinions and share those opinions on your website.

There are companies around such as Trust Pilot or Reviews.co.uk that will manage online reviews on your behalf. The service is pretty good and it can be fairly useful, but be warned, you'll need to pay them for using their platform and it can be quite expensive so be careful. I know that Trust Pilot are willing to discount, so if you're looking to use them, barter very hard and you'll be able to negotiate a decent deal.

I love online reviews I think they're great. They show potential customers that we're serious about our business and that other people have used us and were happy with their services. In their purest form online reviews are a very genuine sample of what people say about our business. It's about as honest an appraisal as any you can get and they can make or break a business. But get something wrong and you'll soon find just how sharp a double-edged sword they can be – a few bad reviews, often from the least expected places, and you can watch your sales figures plummet.

When you're dealing with thousands of orders, you are occasionally going to get it wrong. You just are, so accept it. We've had times in the past where we've posted the wrong item to the buyer, for instance. Of course it's never quite that simple, it'll inevitably be the item they needed for their kids' school play or a special surprise and now we've got it wrong and the occasion is ruined. With some justification the customer is on the phone fuming and it's up to you to do your best to calm them down and resolve the situation. Keep a steady voice and a clear head and, believe me, it can be done.

What's interesting though is that it's not these customers that leave bad feedback. No, it'll be the one who's upset because the shade of blue on the product is just a little darker than it appears to be in the picture. It could be that a different batch is a tone lighter or darker, but it could also be they have the brightness set too high or low on their computer screen, but you'll get a stinging email or snarly phone call and they'll leave you a one star on the review site saying how all your images are inaccurate.

Be prepared, it does happen, but I'm pleased to report that on the whole, the vast majority of people are honest and fair and you'll soon build up a good number of positive and helpful reviews, which will go a long way to showing that you're a serious and professional business.

In fact there is a school of thought that says criticism is the perfect opportunity to really show what your company is all about. How you handle the knockers will say a great deal about your attitude to your customers and the way you run your business. It's a chance to really shine – so take it with both hands!

THREE TOP TIPS

DO
Talk to your customers as much as you can. Use social media, reply to emails and pick up the phone. It's all about building relationships.

A PITFALL
It's easy to fall into the trap of always trying to sell. If you take a genuine interest in what your customers are doing and invest time getting to know them the sales will follow in due course.

DON'T
Forget about your existing customers. It's great to be chasing new ones, but your biggest asset is your existing customer base.

Chapter 8: Get Social

In this chapter:

- **Building an attractive and effective social media profile**

- **Discovering what works best on Facebook, Twitter, Instagram, YouTube etc**

- **Finding out about the unexpected benefits**

Social media has really taken off in the last few years, so much so that most companies now have Facebook and Twitter pages, as well as an Instagram presence for photos, and with video really starting to lead the way in online marketing YouTube is increasingly a must-have in any sales strategy you put together.

It's important to always be consistent across all platforms when it comes to marketing, both digital and physical. Make sure your business has a uniform presence by using the same typefaces, layout styles and colours. You have to be absolutely rigid about this – Coca Cola doesn't use any old red for its logo, it uses Coca Cola red. And its typeface is very specific as well – it's called Spencerian Script and dates from the mid-19th century. Both are absolutely essential to the Coca Cola brand and woe-betide anyone who messes with them.

Check out the Facebook colour palette online as well, there are four shades of blue and one of white, all accompanied by lines of numbers, letters and symbols. They are not for discussion they are the Facebook colour palette. The Facebook font, by the way, is a custom typeface created by a font designer called Joe Kral.

The point is, just as you take care over the way you look to the world, so you must ensure your business looks presentable and consistent. That's how you establish your business as a brand and it is crucial to your success.

Once you've got the look right, you need to get the message out there. This is where social media comes into it's own. Far more direct and completely instant, it is the perfect way to market your business in the modern world. Facebook is great for general messages about your company, as well as offers and deals; whereas Twitter is better for delivering a short message quickly and getting it passed around. YouTube, on the other hand, is more about giving your customers a deeper insight into what you do and where you do it.

It won't be long before you discover that your fans, friends and followers on these various platforms will want to talk to you about your posts, your business and your products. It should come as no surprise, but social media is just that – it's very sociable!

People will often turn to Facebook or Twitter to ask you about your products or your prices. They'll want to know more about things, they might ask about your prices, your shipping arrangements, in fact enquiries through social media could be about anything under the sun.

When people do get in touch with you through social media, make sure you reply immediately – and by immediately I mean right now! In the world of social media an hour is like a day, so don't keep people waiting. If you're managing your social media channels yourself, get the Facebook and Twitter apps installed on your smartphone so that you've always got instant access to any messages wherever you are.

We all love to get positive feedback, but you should be prepared to take to the bad with the good. As hard as you try to get it right, sometimes you're going to mess up and a customer is going to complain. And when they complain through social media it's not like getting an angry phone call or a stinging letter or email, it is by definition very public and potentially very damaging.

An upset customer may very well jump straight onto Twitter and start tweeting you about how you've let them down and how angry they are. Fair enough. Both might be true and in any case, if that's how they feel then they're entitled to feel that way. However, it's very important that you remember not to take this onslaught personally. Do not, under any circumstances, get into an argument with a customer and if you find the communication going that way, do not try to win an argument with your customer. The simple truth is that even if you win the argument, you'll lose the customer.

Instead, keep a cool head, be calm and address their complaint in a professional way as you would if they were stood in front of you. It doesn't matter how wrong they are, how angry they get or how rude, you must remain polite at all times. Social media is a very public arena and nobody benefits by reading a disagreement played out for all to see. What's the old adage? Oh yes, don't wash your dirty linen in public. With social media, once you've typed something online it's there to stay... forever.

The key is to think about it before you post anything on a public forum. You have to remember it is your business you are representing, not your personal self, so act accordingly.

There have been a few disasters in the past on Twitter due to poor reactions from companies to problems or complaints. A major one was when Blackberry went down and nobody could make calls. The people managing the Blackberry Twitter account didn't know about this and went about their normal happy tweets. Obviously they were hit with a barrage of abuse about the poor service, compounded by the fact that Blackberry apparently didn't even know there was an issue.

It took some major backtracking and public grovelling to put that to rights – and if you were one of those affected by the outage it's quite likely that you still harbour some reservations about Blackberry and its ability to keep you connected.

In any other circumstances catching a virus is bad news, but in the social mediasphere it is the best news you can get. Viral is a word that has a very different meaning in social media. You want your posts to go viral. This basically means that, for whatever reason, many hundreds if not thousands of people re-tweet your post. Ideally you want the reason to be a positive one, perhaps a great piece of customer service or a very funny joke, but even less positive tweets can be good – at least it is getting the name of your business out there.

Unfortunately, despite what the clever-clever e-marketing gurus will tell you, there's no recipe for tweets that go viral. What they will say – and I have to agree with them on this – if you get it right a tweet going viral can have a massively positive effect on your company and its sales.

Facebook is the Google of the social media world. It seems that almost everyone on the planet has a Facebook account these days and not only that, but they seem to spend most of their day dropping in and out of their profile, reading updates from friends and family. People lead their lives in plain view of their followers – if they've done it, it's on Facebook and everyone knows about it.

Even though Facebook has had a lot of bad press over recent years due to various privacy concerns, it hasn't stopped everyone sharing aspects of their life ranging from pictures of their pets to more personal subjects such as relationships, or the lack of them. Facebook is an incredibly powerful tool and we are still learning how to live with it in our lives.

People have tried selling products and services via Facebook for many years now, but it has never really taken off, at least not on the scale that the search engines can supply paying customers. However, with the dramatic increase in shopping on mobile platforms and the fact that most people have smartphones and are always logged into their Facebook account, sharing news about your purchases via the platform is easier than ever.

Most website platforms will have modules you can install that will allow your customers to like and share products on your website, but you can also get them to instantly share what they have bought. This is a tremendous opportunity to reward your customers for their purchases because these modules can often be set up in a way so that if the buyer shares their purchase, it unlocks a discount code for their next visit for example. And that's a great way to get them to come back. When these sales are shared on Facebook, friends of that person can then like the post which in turn exposes it to their friends and so on, a nice snowball effect.

You can even get a Facebook shop. There are various companies providing Facebook apps that allow you to list your items for sale, directly on Facebook. Shopping on Facebook is something of an unknown quantity as I don't think either customers or traders have really got to grips with it yet, but I think it's well worth getting a Facebook shop up and running so that you're ready to take advantage of it when it does.

Twitter is more instant, more about the moment. You have a thought, you share a tweet it's that quick. It's a great way to engage your customers regularly and routinely without bombarding them with information or sales messages. Having said that, recently Amazon has been experimenting with the hash tag (#) as a way of adding products to your Amazon cart via the Twitter platform. It's early days, but you can be sure if Amazon is working on it, it's worth having a look at it for your business as well.

We use Twitter to promote special offers and to remind people about key seasonal times of the year such as

Easter, Halloween, Christmas and Valentine's Day. We've got quite a few celebrity followers such as Kelly Hoppen (BBC Dragon's Den), Rachel Elnaugh (former BBC Dragon) and Sam Fairs (TOWIE). They have many thousands of followers so getting a re-tweet from one of these can really help promote the brand and boost sales.

My advice with Twitter would be to follow other people that are of interest to you, or people you think would interest your customers. Don't just pick anyone it won't help in the long run. Once you've started following someone engage in topical conversations that are in some way connected to your line of business and try to introduce what you do to the conversation. Again, there's no need to be heavy handed with the sales messages, but over time you'll build up an active group of followers that are willing to interact with you. It's all about quality not quantity on Twitter.

Instagram is all about pictures and tagging those pictures so that interested people can find them. To be honest, although I'm fully convinced of the platform's benefits I've yet to really embrace the possibilities presented by Instagram – much to our loss I'm sure. For this reason my advice is obviously limited here, but I would suggest you set up an account, if only to secure your business name.

What I know for certain is that Facebook bought Instagram, so there must be something to it. It can also boast more than 200 million active monthly users so there's plenty of opportunity and it is certainly an area that I am going to explore over the coming months.

Many of the world's biggest brands are on Instagram, but it is also hugely popular with small businesses because of the way it encourages creative use of photos. The more creative you are on Instagram the more positive comments you attract and the more shares you'll get. There's no monetisation on Instagram, but users share information, which of course is of interest – and value – to the marketing industry.

Beyond that, Instagram has become a popular way of promoting deals and offers and operates in a similar way to Twitter by using the hash tag. In fact, if you think of it as a visual Twitter you'll be some way to understanding it. Post behind-the-scenes photos from product development, launches, video shoots, offers prizes and discounts related to that product and you'll soon develop a loyal Instagram community.

YouTube is about moving pictures, video. I'm sure you've all used YouTube to search for clips of your favourite songs or scenes from the movies and excerpts of classic television episodes – it's great fun and a pretty cool way to lose an afternoon!

Video is a huge area online right now and with broadband speeds getting faster by the day, YouTube offers the biggest opportunity for online sales we've seen for a long time.

A video is a great way to demonstrate products or for you to talk directly to your visitors. How many times have you got something home and you're not sure how it works, or maybe there's a job you've got to do but you don't really know where to start, YouTube is a brilliant way to establish your expertise by posting how-to videos that promote your business and its goods and services.

Related to that, but subtly different, one area that has really exploded recently is video blogging, or vlogging. Basically, it's where a person makes a video in which they talk about a subject, product or service. It could be in the form of a review or an unboxing and set up guide, but video blogs are a great way of getting specific products right in front of your target audience, usually for free.

There are professional bloggers out there that do this for a living. Just as you would have done with the old-fashioned trade or consumer press, you send them your product for free and they demonstrate it on their profile and offer some opinions about it. Video blogs can get in excess of a million views, but more typically will have a few thousand views per video. The blogger gets to keep the product and you get a few extra sales and some brand exposure to people that are keen enough on your industry to be watching a video blog about it in the first place.

It's worth making contact with the best of these video bloggers. They are enthusiasts in that they run their blogs because they are passionate about their area of expertise and the best of them can exert some serious power over your industry so treat them with a degree of respect as they could benefit your business.

Do a Google search for bloggers in your chosen sector and drop them an email, they may be very busy and could miss one email so don't be afraid of sending a few. Try tweeting them also to get their attention. In our magic business we sponsor some amateur magicians. We send them a certain value of free product each month and they promote us via their social networks, it puts our business directly in front of other magicians, which is perfect for us.

There are many other different social networks out there, but the ones I've discussed here are the main ones. That's not to say that they would be the most successful for you, some of the more obscure ones are focused on very narrow demographics so they might generate higher returns for you.

The key with social media is to get ahead of the competition, try new things, lead the way. As always, take the best of what your competitors are doing, but always look beyond that for the new pastures that they haven't discovered yet – that's what will keep you growing.

Think of your social media accounts as your annual office party, somewhere that you should be having fun. And business should be fun, otherwise what's the point?

One thing that never ceases to amaze me in business, or in life for that matter, is that there really are no wrong steps. Whatever you do has a benefit of some kind somewhere. It could be a fresh idea that opens a new stream of revenue, it might just be a lesson that will save you time and money in the future, but all you need to do is to be tuned in to the possibility of that benefit occurring somewhere in your life and take the time to notice what's happening in your business.

Take this book for example. During the course of writing it I hit on a whole new idea that's basically an extension of my core business. I have built up a wealth of knowledge about starting a business online, then establishing it, maintaining it, marketing it and growing it. I'm not blowing my own trumpet – well, not much anyway – but there's a hell of a lot to learn and I know enough to know it can be pretty daunting to someone who has not operated in this field before.

I didn't have a problem and in many ways that's the reason I wrote the book. I always say to people that I found it incredibly easy to set up a business online because I did. It's not a lie. Maybe my brain just happens to be wired that way, but there it is.

Now, not everyone is going to find it that straightforward, so why don't I offer a service that helps them get started? I didn't want to turn myself into some fancy-pants agency that promises to deliver the moon on a stick and charges you a fortune not to, I wanted to offer simple, easy-to-understand, practical advice to get people started in the wonderful world of e-commerce.

That's how my "Business In A Box" operation began. It's a range of products aimed at business start ups in which I build a business from scratch, create their online presence and teach them how to manage their new digital assets, use e-marketing effectively and get trading.

Basically, if you come to me and say you want to start a business online, I'll ask you what your business is and what it's called, then go away and set it all up for you. Having done that I'll be able to teach you how to maintain your website, update your social media platforms and help you understand the importance of email communication in building valuable customer relations.

A word here about the importance of getting things like design, image and the words you use absolutely right. Your online presence needs to be a reflection of your business, so the images you use, the design of your logo, your branding, your colours and typefaces, everything needs to fit in with what you want to say about your business as a brand. Equally, the words you use to describe your goods and services could be the difference between making a sale and losing a customer, so spend a bit of time thinking about how you want to look online and what you want to say, then seek out the help and advice of experienced professionals.

Having done all that and once I've got your digital business up and running there will still be a point of contact between my business and yours as you are bound to run into problems to solve, or you'll need to look at refreshing your online presence as you update and maintain your assets. As I said, there's a great deal to learn but I enjoy teaching and get a real buzz from seeing what others can achieve with that knowledge.

And the strange thing is I didn't realise any of that before I started writing this book.

What the successful launch of Business In A Box has taught me is that if you put the energy and creativity into one area of your business, the reward for doing so may well come out somewhere else. I've no idea if writing this book will help me sell more fancy dress or magic products online, but the thought that has gone into it and the momentum that has generated has already seen a new business take shape and start to grow.

Isn't that an amazingly powerful thing?

You can apply that in any area of your business – make the effort and stay tuned because you never know where the benefit is going to pop up!

THREE TOP TIPS

DO
Get on Facebook, Twitter and Instagram. These platforms give you a great way to get to know your customers and for them to get to know you.

A PITFALL
It's very easy to take complaints personally, especially when you're a very small company. Be professional, understand the complaint and do your utmost to solve the problem. Every complaint you solve is helping your business be better at whatever it does.

DON'T
Be all about business. Have fun with what you do, this is what will get you through the tough times – of which there will be many.

Chapter 9: Analyse This, Analyse That

In this chapter:

- **Why Google Analytics might just save your business life**

- **Measure everything, interpret the results, then take actions to influence those numbers**

- **Using Google AdWords to boost your business**

You're in business, you're up and running, making sales, shipping orders, getting busy on the social media and generally everything seems perfect. Great. You've always wanted a business and now you've got one. Terrific. Time to relax now, right?

Wrong. In fact, it's very wrong. And here's why.

Ask yourself this one simple question – how do you know your business is working? Unless you're measuring your success in some way, you can never know exactly what's happening. It's one thing to look at your bank statement and see you've got more than you had before, but that's not really going to help going forward.

I'm not the first to say it and I'm not going to be the last, but that doesn't make it any less true – if you can measure it, you can improve it. Luckily, there's a fantastic way to monitor how many people visit your website and what they do while they're on it. It's called

Google Analytics and if you're serious about having a successful online business, you'll need to sign up to this.

Once you have an account with Google (it's free!), all you need to do to enable Google Analytics is put a small piece of code into your website. If you're not sure how to do this, someone you know will be able to help – hell, contact me and I'll do it for you, however you must get it done, just get it done.

Once it is up and running you can then log into a control panel, which gives you all sorts of important and revealing statistics. You can view what's happening live on your site – how many visitors, what country/town they're in, if they're checking out. You'll be able to see how many people have hit your site, where they're coming to your site from, what pages they visit, what they buy, where they go next, how long it takes for them to purchase something, how often do they return, all kinds of fascinating and potentially valuable information relating to your online performance.

This data is absolutely vital, although obviously some bits are more relevant than others. For example, one of the main things you want to monitor when selling online is your conversion rate. If 1,000 people visit your site and 10 of them buy something that would be a 1% conversion rate. Many things affect this number and it'll take you some time to figure out what works best for you and your products or services. You'll probably hit somewhere between 1% and 3% as an average.

Your conversion rate dropping is often the first sign that something is wrong with your business that you need to be aware of. Every business has a degree of seasonal variations, regular peaks and troughs, but on the whole if you find that your conversion rate suddenly taking a dive something is wrong and you should investigate it immediately and don't stop until it recovers.

In our early days selling online I remember logging in one morning and the sales were a bit low, but I put it down to the weather or some other factor and didn't think too much of it. It was only later that evening, when I discovered the sales were still very low that I discovered our SSL certificate – the technology that creates an encrypted connection between your web server and your visitors' web browser to enable sensitive information such as credit card details to be transmitted securely – had expired and everyone trying to checkout was getting a big warning message about our website not being secure.

Given that around 70% of online shoppers have said they have terminated an online order because they didn't trust the transaction, that was potentially disastrous for our business. It was a simple, schoolboy error, but it happens. That's why now, whenever there's a slight drop, I always investigate until the issue is fixed and the cause is known so we can make sure it doesn't happen again.

It's very important to know who is visiting your website and what they're looking at during their visit. Demographics is a word that you probably don't use much in your day-to-day life. I know I didn't, but understanding what they mean and how they have an impact on your sales is key.

Basically, demographics are the statistical data of a population. In other words, the age, gender, number and location of a body of people, in this case the visitors to your website. Understanding the demographics of your visitors puts you in a position to tailor your pages to better appeal to the people visiting your site. In short, getting a firm grip of these statistics will improve your sales.

You'll be surprised to find that certain things that you thought to be true about your customers are probably not true at all. Never assume anything. There is so much data available to you via Google Analytics and all for free, you'd be an absolute fool to not use it. Google Analytics really comes into its own once you have been online for a longer period of time. We often look back over the past three years of data to see the trends and track how we're improving over time. You'll also be able to predict busy times, quiet times and so on. I cannot emphasise enough the importance of using this data. I spend at least an hour every day, looking over these statistics. They are more than just numbers. This information represents exactly what's happening on your website right now and you'll be surprised just how big an asset it will be to your business.

For instance, it's a great way to plan what stock to buy for busy periods of the year. A quick look at Google Analytics and I can see sales figures broken down into specific lines and within those lines the figures are further broken down into buyers. Let's say that last July we sold 234 nun costumes to 200 different buyers. We can sit down and plan our ordering for this coming July knowing with a fair degree of certainty that we're going to need about the same number, plus a few more to allow for growth.

Time after time I see the same patterns, year after year, it's almost spooky how every month will follow the same peaks and troughs as the previous year.

Knowing the statistics is one thing, but if you don't take action then it's wasted knowledge. On our fancy dress website we had a page that was where most people would initially land on our site, yet would lead to the fewest conversions. We put a banner on that page, with a discount code and the conversions increased. It sounds simple now – and it was pretty simple – but without Google Analytics we'd never have known in the first place. Actually, it's more than that. Google Analytics was able to reveal a problem, it's our understanding of that problem and interpretation of the data, coupled with a bit of creative thinking that resulted in a tiny expansion of the business.

I think the lesson here is to get involved with the numbers, play with the data and spot the patterns. Once you have a grasp of what people are doing when they get to your site, then you need to think like a shopper and you should be able to increase your sales in many different ways.

Here's a suggestion you might like to try. Take a look at your Google Analytics account and pull up the statistics for the last 90 days. Compare this to the same 90 days in the previous year if you have that data. You'll see that each day/week/month will follow the same pattern as the previous year. So if you're growing then you'll see at what rate. The way to use this data would be to take it and drop it onto the same 90-day period next year, applying the same rate of growth that you had achieved over the previous year.

This is a great way to forecast sales, which will be of enormous help should you ever need to apply for a loan for example. The forecast is based on actual achieved sales not just made up numbers based on the way the wind was blowing that day.

Security is a vital component of shopping online. We've all seen the horror stories on the news of identity theft and credit card fraud. The truth of the matter is that with some basic precautions, you can protect yourself and visitors to your website quite easily.

The first thing you need when selling online is an SSL (Secure Socket Layer) certificate. This encrypts the transaction information before it is passed to the payment gateway so that it's almost impossible for someone to intercept and decode that info. There are many different companies that provide SSL certificates and a few different levels/types of actual certificate. Prices will range from free to around £500 for a typical website, but there's no need to spend more than £20 or £30 when you're starting out.

However, there are a few things to consider when choosing one.

The best you can get is generally viewed as being an EV (Extended Validation) certificate. To install one of these on your website you'll need to provide the issuer with official documents identifying your company and its address. These are generally quite expensive, around £200-£500, depending on where you buy from.

The benefits can be argued over, but in my view if you're selling more £100,000 of product a year, you should invest in an EV certificate. From the website visitors' point of view they will see the address bar in the browser turn green, such as when you're logged into PayPal or Amazon. It can also have a higher compatibility with a wider range of browsers, eliminating those annoying odd errors when people try to checkout.

One thing that many people forget or often deliberately exclude is the contact details of the business. You have to display your address and contact details by law in the UK, but it also goes a very long way with buyers. If they can see where you are and how to contact you, they are more likely to buy from you.

I never buy from a website if they don't have a real address and a landline phone number displayed clearly on their website, there are plenty of other places for people to spend their money. In fact, now would be a great time for you to evaluate what makes you decide to buy from a website and more importantly what makes you decide to not make a purchase. It's easy to lose sight of the fact that yes, you're the business owner but you're also a shopper.

Google AdWords is the system Google has developed to help you market your goods and services within its search engine by using a text advert that appears when people search for phrases that relate to your offering. The advert appears as a sponsored link with a little yellow 'Ad' box alongside it at the top of the first page of search results. It's a 'pay-per-click' system, which allows you to dictate where your advert appears through bidding for a series of phrases, but you only pay the amount you have bid for if someone clicks on your advert as a result of a web search.

It's pretty effective as well. But as with everything else you have to stay on top of Google AdWords and other shopping ads as they are constantly changing. Almost every year Google cooks up a new way of doing it, even though the core offering stays about the same though.

Here are a few things you'll want to implement on your account.

To get all the basics set up, I suggest you speak to Google on the phone. There's no one better to get you up and running than Google itself. The call will take about an hour on the phone and by the end of it you should have all the basics in place. One thing I would suggest you do first though is to break down your product listing adverts by category.

It's very simple to do. When you're logged into your AdWords account, on the far left click on the campaign that contains your shopping products, then click on your Ad Group. In the centre of the screen where it says "All Products" they will be a + symbol, click this.
Now you'll be able to click the dropdown menu at the top and sub-divide your products by various options such as category and brand. These options are what you placed in your product feed that you uploaded to Google. Once you have saved a sub group you'll be able to set the specific cost-per-click on that group, rather than having to set a price for all your products.

This is great because you may already perform well in certain areas, so there's no need to spend more on those, whereas you may want to promote specific seasonal items and want to allocate a higher spend-per-click.

You can't break this so play around with it before it goes live. There are many options and settings that affect the way your products are displayed and the position they appear in. If you find that you've mucked it all up – and believe me it can easily happen – simply phone Google and they'll straighten it out for you and get you back on track. They're really helpful like that.

In our business we've broken our Ad Groups down by category and by brand. That works really well for us, but find out what works for you.

You can cap your spending on Google ads by setting a maximum daily spend. I would recommend keeping this very low to start with, until you're familiar with the way it all works. Something around £5 a day should give you enough data to see what's working and what's not. After around a month or so, you should be in a position to work out where it will be worth your while increasing your spend, confident that you'll be getting a reasonable return on your investment.

Once you know what you're doing and if you have a popular range of products, you will have no problem spending upwards of £250 a day. Bigger companies will spend in excess of £10,000 a week quite easily.

THREE TOP TIPS

DO
Measure everything – visits, sales, clicks... If you can measure it, you can improve it.

A PITFALL
You may think you know your customers, but I would wager you're wrong. There are tools such as Google Analytics available to help you truly know them – use them.

DON'T
Assume anything. It's your business and you need to know everything.

Chapter 10: The Sun Always Shines On TV

In this chapter:

- **Me and Duncan Bannatyne – be careful what you wish for**

- **Staffing your growing business and how to make money through multiple streams of income**

- **Learn how to recognise the time to sell and making the best exit possible to live your dream**

The world of business is often looked at as an evil dark place, full of heartless greedy people who would sell their own grandmothers to make a profit. This may have been true of the past, but certainly my experience has been the total opposite. Some of the nicest and most caring people I've met are business owners, not at all greedy or selfish people. In fact, I would say that to be a successful business owner, these are traits that you'll need in abundance, along with patience.

That is unless you're a dragon from the TV show Dragons' Den (they're lovely people really). My wife and I, along with a brief appearance from some of our kids, had the dubious pleasure of appearing on the show back in 2011 – series nine, episode three for those of you that are interested in tracking it down to watch it.

If I can call up some of those wavy visual effects now …

I was sat at home in front of my computer around midnight on a cold February night when I stumbled across the application for the show online. What harm could it do, right? So I spent the next couple of hours filling it in and then submitted the thing thinking I'd never hear anything back.

How wrong was I? I was up in Bedworth trying to sort out some issues we had with one of our shops when I took a call from a producer of the show.

"Hi can I speak to Peter please?" they asked. "This is Ben, I'm a producer from BBC's Dragons' Den."

That was the start of a journey that would see our business literally double in size over the next 12 months.

Over the next few weeks there followed a series of phone calls and loads of questions from people at the Beeb until eventually we were invited to the BBC Television Centre at Wood Lane in Shepherds Bush for a screen test. We had to answer more questions, this time on camera, and generally talk about the business. It seemed to go pretty well I thought and sure enough, not long after, they invited us to appear on the show.

The date was set and the nerves really started to mount. My wife and I are not shy people, but there's something about appearing in front of five very successful millionaire business owners, not to mention the millions of viewers at home that makes you doubt your own name, never mind all the statistics and numbers we would need to commit to memory.

As the day drew closer we would practice our pitch over and over again (probably a mistake as it turned out) reading the numbers, profit, debt, sales, turnover, all the stuff that you know on any other day, but the fear of appearing on the show was making it all that much harder.

The day before we were to be filmed, we drove to a hotel near the studios and checked in – two rooms as there was that many of us. So, there we were on the eve of our TV debut, my suit was hanging up, shirt ironed, shoes shined, pitch practiced. We thought that finally we were ready. The kids were very excited about appearing on telly. What could possibly go wrong?

Morning soon came and after a full English and a few cups of coffee, we were off on our way to the studio – it was filmed at Pinewood when we did it, I think it's done up in Manchester these days. Arriving we were greeted by Ben who's a nice chap and worked hard at making us feel welcome.

We got there early as we'd been told to and were duly whisked off to the waiting area or Green Room, as showbiz types like to call it. There were several other people there, waiting for their big moment on the show, all looking very nervous… as were we.

Still, when in Rome and all that, so we helped ourselves to the free fizzy drinks, crisps and chocolate, which helped calm the nerves a bit. Next job was make-up. While my wife was obviously very used to this kind of thing, I wasn't. It felt very odd, although, I have to say any help with regards to my looks is a good thing!

The hours went by until eventually we were called to go to the studio. First though, some more waiting, this time just outside the entrance where we made sure our props were all ready and set up. Then it was time; we were on. Everything we had done from that late night back in February, from applying online to standing outside the infamous Dragons' Den was about to come to a head.

In we walked and there they were. The dragons were all seated, just as you see on screen. The silence in the room was only broken by the sound of us walking across the floor in our shiny new shoes. We pulled back the black cloth from our party table prop (looking back, it was a poor effort from us), looked for the X that marks the spot where we had to stand, took our positions, looked up, drew a deep breath and started our pitch.

We remembered most of what we wanted to say, I think. Time seemed to both stand still and fly by, if that's possible. I know it was a pretty short presentation, but I remember thinking we'd got through that part relatively unscathed.

It was at that moment that the ground was literally pulled from underneath us in one sweeping statement from the ever-lovely Deborah Meaden...

She said it was one of the easiest decisions she had to make with regards to investing in a company and that it was as though we just made it up outside in the car park. She was out. That was it. Everything we had committed to memory was gone. Perhaps that was her intention, to throw us off balance. Who knows?

Then Theo Paphitis decided it was his turn. At one point he was actually out of his chair shouting "No!" at me. He told us our business was doomed to failure and it would never work. They were tough words to hear. He was out and by this time, we thought we knew how it was going to pan out and were pretty much waiting for the rest to take their bite out of us.

As it turned out, Peter Jones was fairly nice about it. He said he thought we were doing OK, but that our future plans for the business were flawed. In fact, he didn't have a go at us at all really, but he was out all the same. Hilary Devey let us off fairly lightly as well although we thought she kind of misunderstood what we were planning to do but let us off fairly lightly.

Then it came to Duncan Bannatyne. Now, Duncan isn't exactly famous for his delicate words as far as being a dragon is concerned, so our loins were girded for a proper grilling.

He said to me: "So, Peter, how do you think it's gone so far?" I remember thinking: 'Are you taking the piss?' but instead I asked: "Can we please start again?" I was joking of course, although had the answer been that we could I would have jumped at the chance.

Anyway, to our surprise he said that he thought we could make a success of franchising the business and mentioned how it had worked with Razzamatazz, a previous investment in the Den. After a few more minutes of discussing the business, he said those all-important words: "Well, I'm going to make you an offer."

That was what we had gone into the Den for, every comment from the other dragons now meant nothing. We went in to get an offer and we were about to get one. Success, right? Well, his offer was £100,000 for 60% of the business. What? 60%? There was no way were we going to accept that. What a cheek.

But he wasn't to be put off and after some negotiating a figure of £100,000 for 50% was agreed and we shook hands on the deal. We'd got what we came for, a deal with a dragon and some exposure on one of the most popular shows on television. These are the moments that are supposed to define your life, we expected to feel as high as kites, yet the victory – if that's what it was – felt distinctly hollow.

The next few months were spent getting the accounts together and answering lots of questions from his team who are nothing if not thorough. It wasn't helped by the fact that we were in the process of changing accountants at the time so that really slowed things down. We submitted all the answers they wanted, then received some more questions about our staff, their contracts and all kinds of things we never saw coming.

In the midst of all that the day came around when our episode was due to be broadcast. Even though we had been worked really hard by Duncan's people and were struggling to make sense of what had happened to us, the thought of seeing ourselves on telly was genuinely exciting. I can feel the buzz again just writing this now.

And it wasn't just just on a personal level either – we expected the business to get a kick out of it as well and

had prepared the website for all the extra traffic we knew it would get.
So there we were, sat waiting for the show to come on, fingers crossed that the editors had been kind to us…

But they hadn't. We came over really badly. I mean really badly, so bad it's hard to imagine how it could have been worse.

To be fair, looking back on it now we know we performed well below par on the day and the editors can only work with the material we gave them so there are no hard feelings. The fact is we were awful. Still, the website went down due to the amount of extra hits it received but not for long – it was back up within 10 minutes. Strangely enough we didn't get a single extra order that night over and above what we would usually have received. I thought that was a very bad sign.

Since then the episode has been repeated many times on TV and each time we see a little spike in orders, so in the long run there has been nothing to complain about on that score.

But back to the offer from Duncan. The due diligence process dragged on and on, taking over a year in the end. By the time all the hoops had been jumped through, the i's dotted and the t's crossed, a full six months had gone by since the show had aired and things were looking up – our business was now growing more rapidly than it had at any point in the past.
Then, once again, the rug was pulled from under our feet. A caveat of Duncan's offer was that our net profit was at a level of around £80,000. It wasn't. Once our accounts were completed, the adjusted figure was much

less so the offer was withdrawn and now Duncan was out as well. That's it. Finished. Over.

I was gutted, to say the least. It was terrible news, a real sickener, but once I'd got over myself, picked myself up and got back into it again I knew everything would be fine. In fact, over the next couple of years, it would prove to not be so bad at all.

It's now more than three years since we appeared in the Den and our business is turning over twice the amount it was, with profits triple what they were back then. The show clearly helped raise our profile and put us firmly on the fancy dress industry map.

We've had the odd email back and forth from Duncan's team since they withdrew the offer, but none of the exchanges has ever led to us doing a deal. I would still consider going into business with him, but I'm lucky enough that our business doesn't need the investment for the time being.

Personally, I doubt their claim that the dragons have no prior knowledge of the people going in to the Den, as a few things were said that kind of gave that away. Maybe once you walk into the Den, they are fed questions through earpieces or something, I don't know, but some of the things that they were saying make me think they are guided in some way or another.

There's no denying the experience was exciting and that excitement was and continues to be really good for the business. Whatever the outcome, the excitement is a reward in itself, it gets the juices flowing, you think better, you feel better and you perform better, it's the lifeblood of the business. I think I need a daily dose of it if I'm honest because it keeps me sharp and helps me focus. The area of e-commerce is constantly changing daily and the things that work for you today, may not work for you tomorrow. This is why it's so important to be ready to adapt, almost at a moment's notice. The businesses that don't adapt fail – and they fail fast.

You have to recognise there will be hard times, business is not all chocolates and roses. But once you know these hard times will come and go, it's a lot easier to get through them. In fact, hard times are characterised by problems and problems are there to be solved. Do yourself a favour and learn to get a creative buzz out of solving problems because it'll stand you in good stead in your business life.

I've found running a business is like growing a plant or raising a pet – you start with something small and in the early stages you have to nurse it through every single step it takes. As it grows it starts to take on a personality of its own; a strength that allows you to take a step back and see it grow. It's a living, breathing thing, with good days and bad. Just like we are. It's your job to give it the space to grow and make money while being there to guide it when the tough times hit.

There are only 24 hours in each day and you can only work so many of them. Even if you work all of them, it's not enough to grow a big business. That means you are going to need to employ people at some point. You're definitely going to need to get someone else to do some of the jobs for you and that either means you sub contract certain elements of the workload, or – more likely because it will save money – bring someone else into the team and keep it in-house.

Now, employing someone is not as easy as you might first think. It's nowhere near as simple as getting your mates in to help out, although that is an option in the early days. But if you're going to do it properly – and I suggest that's the only realistic way of doing anything – you have to pick someone you can trust with your business. You want them on your side so treat them well and reward them fairly.

You also need to be realistic and make sure your expectations are fair. They are working for you, but it's your business not theirs. They will have a life outside of working for you so you can be pretty sure they're not going to be up at 2am toiling over that special order to make you look better. Not unless you make it worth their while.

Then you'll need to negotiate the minefield that is employment law. There is a whole heap of legal obligations and requirements that you need to be aware of. Basic, day one stuff includes pay, holiday allowance, sickness, contracts, maternity and paternity allowances, not to mention health and safety.

And if you're going to hire people you'd better realise you're also going to have to fire people. With that comes another raft of legal stuff, not to mention the emotional pain of having to tell someone you don't need them any more. It's probably one of the worse things you'll ever have to do as a business owner, especially if the person you're letting go is a friend or family member. This will sound like a cliché, but sometimes clichés are created simply because they are true... Business is business and no matter how painful it is for you to tell someone you care about they've got to go, you have to do what is best for the business as a whole. If they've got anything about them they'll realise it's not personal and accept the decision with a bit of dignity. Tread carefully, act with kindness and try to put yourself in their shoes, these decisions are incredibly difficult to make and acting on them is even harder, but they will make your business better and you a better business owner.

Part of getting those decisions right is to make sure you know how to follow the correct legal process and believe me you need a lot of help with the legal stuff. Although there are some very good websites packed with useful information, I would recommend you call on someone you can be sure will have your best interests at heart. It's not the only reason, but it is one of the mains ones, that I recommend you join the Federation of Small Businesses.

This is not the place for me to sell its services to you, but look them up and see what it can do for you and your small business. I've been a member for many years and in my view it's been money well spent.

You'll hear a lot about the merits of networking, the world of small business is awash with groups of people that get together to talk about their businesses to one another. While it's good to know that other people have the same problems as you so you know you're not alone – they may even have come up with different ways of solving similar problems – and it's possible you might be able to swap a few contacts and leads, it's also worth remembering that the more time you spend talking about business, the less time you spend actually doing business.

Employing family has its drawbacks, but it can be a great way to grow your business and it has the added bonus of keeping the assets and the profits close to home. After all, you want to do what you can to improve the lives of those closest to you, right? My business is currently made up of my wife and I at the helm with two of our daughters, Jade and Amie, managing dispatch and customer service, but we couldn't achieve what we do without the help and support of our other team members.

As you employ more people, different rules and laws kick in to play, so keep that in mind when adding to your workforce. We currently have nine employees and it's quite a task to manage payroll, holidays, shifts and training. Get just one of those things wrong and you run the risk of upsetting the people you need to make your business run smoothly. In our situation we have to do all this ourselves, the buck stops firmly with us, it's not like being an employee or a manager for someone else where you can just pick up the phone and talk to the payroll department for instance, it's all down to us.

You'll know pretty quickly when you need to take people on – it's usually just before you realise that not taking people on is actually going to hurt your business because you can't complete orders on time or your standards of service are dropping. However, taking people on is a huge decision and not one to be taken lightly. There are lots of questions to answer. Do you need full-time or part-time staff? Casual labour or permanent staff to train up for more senior roles? How do new people fit in to your existing business structure? How much can you pay? Will you get the best people for that money? How should they work for you?

For instance, home working or remote working is becoming more and more popular. The thinking goes that if someone is relaxed and given the freedom to control their own time, they will be more productive. Now, I'm not sure where I stand on that to be honest. I'm a bit of a control freak in that sense, so I like to know what's going on and see the results, but there are companies that swear by this system and maybe it'll work for your business, but it's an option that deserves consideration at least.

So this is the final chapter of this book, my first book and I really hope you've been able to take some things from it. I don't claim to have all the answers, but I certainly know a lot of the questions and that'll get you started in the right direction.

As I write this I'm in the process of house hunting, not quite a millionaire's mansion, but my journey isn't complete yet. It's important to remember that to have a very comfortable life, you don't need to make millions... and you'll start to have fun and be able to relax long before that point.

There will come a point in your business when you'll have learned your own lessons and found your own shortcuts, that you'll want to replicate it. At this point my advice is stick to what you know. Try to do what you're already doing but tweak it slightly, don't reinvent the wheel as they say.

Try to create lots of smaller revenue streams but never take your eye off your core business, the business that pays the bills.

Nothing lasts forever and that's especially true in the business world. There will come a time that hopefully you'll recognise, when it's time to get out. With a bit of luck and some planning, you may be able to sell your business to another company or individual buyer. Don't undersell what you have. There are people out there with lots of money looking to buy successful businesses, so remember what you have, has value.

It's important if you're going to sell that you do so while there's still money to be made in the business. Staying passionate for years running the same business can be very difficult and you don't want to lose interest and start letting it all fall apart. Remember that dream you had, right back at the beginning, that's what you're doing all this for and never lose sight of that.

So there we have it. Thanks for taking the time to read about my journey and all its ups and downs. I really would like to hear about what you're doing and how you're hoping to achieve your dreams. Send me an email, my details are in the back of this book.

Stay focused, have fun and never lose sight of your goals.

THREE TOP TIPS

DO
Remember you're in business to make money. Once you find something that works, replicate it.

A PITFALL
You can easily get complacent, but nothing lasts forever. You have to keep changing things to keep them fresh and to keep ahead of the competition.

DON'T
Ever lose sight of why you started your business in the first place. Stay completely focused at all times.

Useful Contacts

www.channelunity.com
ChannelUnity is a comprehensive and feature rich solution for online retailers.

www.paypal.com
World leading payment processor.

www.ebay.co.uk
Online market place to sell your products

www.amazon.co.uk
Online market place to sell your products

www.magento.com
ecommerce platform for building your website on.

www.sagepay.com
An alternative payment processor to Paypal.

www.google.com/merchants
Set up your merchant account so that you can manage your Google product feeds.

www.sonassi.com
Magento based websites.

www.wholesaledeals.co.uk & www.alibaba.com
Portals for sourcing wholesale product.

www.themagicoctopus.co.uk
Online marketing and social media management.

www.screwitjustdoit.com
Come and say hi.

So you want to be an author…?

Nothing says you mean business better than a book.

Magic Octopus Publishing specialises in bringing business-related books to market across a range of platforms, including physical and digital formats.

Our authors are leaders in their respective fields, successful in business and, like all truly successful people, they are eager to share what they have learned and pass on what they've learned.

A book is also a priceless marketing tool, a golden opportunity to add value to any business while promoting its services. A book builds public profile, confirms expertise and provides a point of contact.

Magic Octopus Publishing is supported by award winning writers and expert designers to create fantastic titles that will benefit any business.

How it works

We'll work with you to identify a format that will work best for you and your business. It might be a biographical book, explaining how you achieved your success. It might be a book of tips, about how to maintain that success. Your book could make a feature of stunning photography; or it might be more text-based, a personal growth manual perhaps?

The book will establish your credibility within the industry and in business generally by revealing your career highlights, mentioning any specific results, awards, innovations or notable high points that set you apart from others in your field.

Your books will be informative and well segmented, using anecdotes, examples and real-life cases to make points. Readers want to know about your business and how your experience will help them in their own business, but they also want to know about you. The more they can identify with you the more likely they are to pay attention to your advice and change their own lives accordingly.

It's important that your book is exactly that – *your* book. Our writers have years of experience as authors and journalists and can provide as much or as little input as you want, but the book must deliver your message as clearly as possible.

Once you've approved the content, again in consultation with our writers, the book is then sent for design. There follows a process of draft and revision until you are happy with the completed publication, which is then uploaded to the Kindle store and sent off to print.

Magic Octopus Publishing also provides a first rate marketing service. We design, build, test and launch a range of eye-catching digital assets related to the book including a website, social media platforms and email campaigns. **www.octopuspublishing.co.uk**

www.ingramcontent.com/pod-product-compliance
Lightning Source LLC
Chambersburg PA
CBHW060854170526
45158CB00001B/358